Lumière

ROB FEENIE

LUMIÈRE

FOREWORD BY CHARLIE TROTTER

TEN SPEED PRESS

BERKELEY·TORONTO

This book is dedicated to my parents,

Laurie and Margaret Feenie, for their

support, patience and a huge amount of

understanding, and to Sherri Morrison for

being there through it all and to everyone

else who decided to believe.

Ten Speed Press
Box 7123
Berkeley, California 94707
www.tenspeed.com

Originated by Douglas & McIntyre
2323 Quebec Street, Suite 201
Vancouver, British Columbia
Canada v5t 4s7

Editing by Elizabeth Wilson and Lucy Kenward
Cover and text design by Peter Cocking
Photography by John Sherlock
Food styling by Nathan Fong
Printed and bound in Hong Kong by C&C Offset
Printed on acid-free paper ∞

Library of Congress Cataloging-in-Publication Data:
On file with publisher

First printing, 2002

1 2 3 4 5 6 7 8 9 10 — 06 05 04 03 02

Contents

Foreword

IN EACH GENERATION of young chefs, only a handful really understand the groundwork laid by those who have come before them. They do not just pay lip service to the tenets, but they fully ingest, read, study, savor and labor over the cuisine created by the masters of previous generations. Rarer still are new chefs who use that hard-earned culinary education to express their own creativity and heritage. In a time when it is common for chefs to simply reproduce the innovations of others, the few who speak for themselves through their food become the skilled artists of their time. These chefs will inspire creativity and excellence in the chefs around them and raise the bar for those who follow. Robert Feenie is such a chef.

I first met Rob through a mutual friend who is a great lover of food and wine. The passion and dedication Rob showed from the minute he entered the restaurant immediately endeared this young chef to me, and we quickly became friends. Since that first meeting, he has visited our restaurant on several occasions, often spending time working in the kitchen. The staff thoroughly enjoy his visits because his immense knowledge and stature never interfere with his quest to learn and experience all things new. He does not hesitate to jump in alongside the cooks and dig his hands into whatever work needs to be done. This zeal has served him well, helping him to become a culinary force. When he asked me to write the foreword for his book, I quickly answered a resounding "Yes!" Upon receiving the advance copy of the book, I was even more delighted to sing its praises. Rob's unquenchable thirst for excellence permeates everything he does.

This book is a joy—the viewer senses the undeniable joy that Rob brings to each page. It is a pleasure—the cook feels the infectious pleasure that infuses each recipe and its description. It is a love—the reader perceives the true labor of love that resulted in this wonderful volume. Rob lets his vibrant personality and unique perspective shine through-out the book. Only a Canadian could pen such a telling line as: "Learning to season in cooking is like learning to stickhandle in hockey; it's absolutely fundamental." Only Rob could so unabashedly describe summer as "the freedom and exuberance of childhood" and spring as "an abundance and a full palette of green."

The dishes illustrate Rob's brilliant artistry with the best foods of each season. Summer comes alive in his Seared Scallops with Green Pea Ravioli and a Summer Truffle Butter Sauce. This heady combination brings together the bright flavors of new produce, the sweetness of fresh shellfish and the earthiness of truffles. Without even entering the kitchen, the reader cannot help but salivate.

His Sake and Maple Marinated Sablefish with a Citrus and Soy Sauce speaks to Rob's Canadian heritage. Sable, which is native to Canada and alternatively known as black cod, is a luscious fish that borders on decadent. The citrus salad garnish perfectly complements the richness of the fish, bringing acidity without excessive tartness. Rob then throws in a bit of the Asian influence found in British Columbia with the soy sauce in the glaze. That dash truly completes the dish and makes it his own.

Cooks and diners alike will also delight in this book's wonderful treatment of the cheese course—a cause I heartily endorse. Through his thoughtful discussion of what in Europe is a fundamental part of the meal, Rob makes cheese service less daunting for North Americans. He offers innovative suggestions and simple tips for including this savory course in any dinner party. Such additions, as well as several helpful explanations, ensure the success of every culinary enterprise undertaken with this book in hand.

In fact, I am hoping to steal a few ideas from the book myself. . . .

CHARLIE TROTTER

Introduction

FIVE YEARS AGO I opened Lumière because I had something to say. For me, food is conversation. Why and what I cook are my passions and beliefs, shared with anyone who cares to listen.

Growing up, I listened to my mother's food and heard it tell me how much she cared. It was a language I wanted to speak.

After hearing poetry in the food of Sweden and France as a teenager, I went to school for a basic vocabulary. There I learned just how hard poetry can be. It takes discipline and technique. When I played hockey as a kid, I hated practice. I just wanted to play. When I left school, I just wanted to cook.

Michel Jacob, at Le Crocodile in Vancouver, hired me. I listened to his food and it told me about discipline. He taught me to practice. Then I went to Alsace to hear Emile Jung's and Antoine Westermann's gorgeous dishes, and they taught me about technique. I was learning to speak French. The problem was, I didn't know if anyone wanted to listen.

The question was answered when I went to Charlie Trotter's in Chicago. Listening to his food brought me an epiphany. His food spoke French, American and all the other tongues, but it came together in a language all his own. Charlie and his food gave me the confidence to let my food speak its mind, and showed me the possibilities that could result.

I hope my food speaks the French I love, the Japanese and Chinese I hear around me in Vancouver and the Canadian I am. I hope that my food speaks to you.

ROB FEENIE

{ S P R I N G }

I REMEMBER looking out of my window on a warm spring morning when I was a kid

and thinking, "I wish the rest of the world knew about this place." Vancouver truly is one of

the prettiest cities in the world, and in spring it explodes—thousands of blossoming pink

trees, huge clusters of daffodils and giant rhododendrons everywhere look like something

out of the tropical jungles. Everybody comes out of hibernation and heads outside.

It's an exciting time in the restaurant. Now we can buy local again. Friendships are

renewed as the growers phone to tell us what's available, and soon we're seeing lettuces,

herbs, asparagus, morels, fava beans and strawberries freshly picked that day. After having

to be resourceful through the winter months, spring suddenly brings abundance and a full

palette to create with. The cooking shifts to complement the delicacy of the flavors, and

I can once again indulge my taste for food that's airy, light and refined.

Spring

Young garlic velouté soup   5

White and green asparagus salad with a
warm soy and truffle vinaigrette   7

Spring vegetable ragout with wild
mushroom consommé   13

Duo des pommes de terre   10

Brillat-Savarin cheese with strawberries
and balsamic glaze   30

Pink grapefruit sorbet with
gin and vanilla jus   176, 179

Lemon and buttermilk panna cotta with
a blueberry compote   37

SIGNATURE MENU

Napoleon of Dungeness crab with
curry mayonnaise and a pineapple and
celery broth   *18*

Seared foie gras with sundried
tomato chutney   *28*

Tuna tartare with tamari vinaigrette   *19*

Goat cheese ravioli with a
light curry froth   *14*

Braised halibut casserole with wild
mushrooms and black truffle butter   *22*

Poached free-range chicken breast with a
morel and white asparagus cream   *26*

Roasted rack of lamb with a casserole of
spring vegetables and rosemary oil   *27*

Le Coutances cheese with a mixed
apple napoleon   *33*

Pink champagne and cherry granité   *176*

Lime curd Pavlova with a coconut
citrus sauce   *38*

SEAFOOD MENU

Garganelli pasta with spot prawns and
a lemon and thyme butter sauce   *17*

Chilled purée of English pea soup
with crème fraîche and caviar   *6*

Poached wild spring salmon with
baby artichokes, capers, niçoise olives
and roasted red peppers   *20*

Sake and maple marinated sablefish with
a citrus and soy sauce   *25*

Valençay cheese with a
warm beet salad   *31*

Strawberry granité with
mint jus   *177, 179*

Chocolate tango cake with bittersweet
chocolate sorbet   *34*

Young garlic velouté soup (facing)

Young garlic velouté soup

1 lb. young pearl garlic

2 cups whole milk

6 Tbsp. unsalted butter

2 large yellow onions, finely chopped

1½ stalks celery, finely chopped

3 sprigs fresh tarragon, plus 1 sprig
   for garnish

6 cups chicken stock or vegetable stock
   (see pages 169 or 170)

1 large Yukon Gold potato, peeled and
   coarsely chopped

2 cups heavy cream

lemon juice, to taste

enoki mushrooms for garnish

ABOUT THE RECIPE: Young garlic is available in the spring but if unavailable, use elephant garlic, which has a similar mild flavor. Pearl garlic is also mild. It's the kind where the entire bulb is one clove. If none of these is available, use regular garlic poached an additional 5 minutes in milk.

TO PREPARE: Peel garlic and remove germ in center. Immerse garlic cloves in boiling water and blanch for 3 minutes. Remove garlic from boiling water and immerse in cold water; peel.

Bring milk and peeled garlic to a simmer in a large saucepan over medium heat. Poach garlic in milk for 5 minutes. Strain and remove garlic.

Heat 2 Tbsp. of the butter in a large pot over medium-high heat. When melted, add poached garlic, onion, celery, tarragon, stock, potatoes, salt and freshly ground white pepper. Bring to a boil; reduce heat and simmer until potatoes are cooked well. Add cream and bring just to a boil. Remove from heat.

Remove tarragon from soup and discard. Purée soup in a blender or food processor and strain through a fine sieve. Return to pot. Adjust seasoning with salt, freshly ground white pepper and lemon juice. Adjust consistency with stock if necessary. Stir in the remaining 4 Tbsp. butter, a little at a time, until incorporated.

To serve, divide soup among bowls, sprinkle on some snipped tarragon leaves and float a few enoki mushrooms on top.

WINE: A medium-bodied New World Chardonnay.

Serves 6 to 8

Chilled purée of English pea soup with crème fraîche and caviar

4 cups water
1 cup sugar
½ cup sea salt
3 cups fresh or frozen English peas
½ cup vegetable or chicken stock
   (see page 170 or 160)

½ cup water
lemon juice, to taste
crème fraîche for garnish
caviar, such as beluga or osetra,
   for garnish

ABOUT THE RECIPE: This soup was on the menu at Lumière when we opened, and has long since become one of my personal favorites because it is so fresh and full of flavor.

To get that really pure pea flavor, I use vegetable stock and water rather than a stronger-tasting chicken stock. I also like to serve this the same day it is made. Some soups taste better the next day because of oxidation, but with this one, the flavor and color will diminish with time. Warm or cold, this classic soup is stunning.

TO PREPARE: Bring the 4 cups water, sugar and salt to a boil. Immerse the green peas in the boiling water no longer than 2–3 minutes (if using frozen, blanch no more than 1 minute). Plunge the peas into ice water so that they can chill as quickly as possible. Drain.

Purée the peas in a food processor. Press the purée through a fine-mesh sieve with the back of a spoon, or pass it through a food mill. This step is a fair bit of work but well worth it in the end. You should have about 2 cups of the pea purée.

Blend the pea purée, vegetable stock and the ½ cup water in small batches. If you prefer a thicker soup, add more purée. If you prefer a thinner soup, add more vegetable stock. Add lemon. Transfer to an airtight container and chill in the refrigerator until ready to serve.

To serve, season the soup with salt to taste. Ladle the soup among the serving bowls, garnish with a dollop of crème fraîche and top with caviar.

WINE: A Sauvignon Blanc.

Serves 4 · photo, page 48

White and green asparagus salad with a warm soy and truffle vinaigrette

VINAIGRETTE

2 Tbsp. light soy sauce

1 Tbsp. rice vinegar or truffle vinegar

1 Tbsp. fresh lemon juice

5 Tbsp. extra virgin olive oil

½ Tbsp. truffle oil

½ tsp. finely chopped fresh black truffle

1 lb. green asparagus

1 lb. white asparagus

5 cups microgreens or mesclun greens

ABOUT THE RECIPE: White asparagus always takes me back to when I was training in Alsace. White asparagus is served everywhere there, not just in the high-end restaurants. Because it is grown under the soil, it has no color and its flavor is more subtle than that of green asparagus.

Asparagus is at its peak from spring to the beginning of summer. The easiest way to tell if asparagus is past its prime is to look at the bottoms of the stalks. If they are dried out and beginning to shrivel, the stalks have been out of water too long and will be tough and fibrous when cooked. Always make sure that the bottoms are moist and freshly cut.

TO PREPARE: In a small pot, combine soy sauce, vinegar, lemon juice and freshly ground white pepper. Bring to a simmer; remove pot from heat and whisk in olive oil and truffle oil. When ready to serve, gently warm the vinaigrette and stir in truffles.

For green asparagus, snap off the fibrous ends. Peel the stalks if you prefer a more elegant look. White asparagus should be peeled and 1 inch trimmed from the bottom. White asparagus is not as flexible as green and will break easily if not handled gently.

Bring 2 large pots of salted water to a boil. Place the green asparagus in one and cook uncovered for 3–4 minutes until tender but still firm and bright green. Immediately plunge stalks into ice-cold water to stop the cooking.

Place the white asparagus in the other pot and allow to simmer uncovered for 4 minutes. Remove the pot from heat and allow asparagus to sit in the hot water for another 3 minutes. Plunge stalks into ice-cold water. Asparagus can be rewarmed at serving time by blanching for 30 seconds in boiling salted water or microwaving for 20 seconds.

TO ASSEMBLE: Have both vinaigrette and asparagus warm. Divide the asparagus among 4 large plates. Mix the microgreens with some of the warm vinaigrette and season with salt and freshly ground white pepper. Place the greens on top of the asparagus. Spoon some of the remaining vinaigrette around each plate and serve.

WINE: A white Bordeaux or style thereof, a Semillon Sauvignon blend with judicious oak.

Serves 4

A note on serving sizes

These recipes make smaller than normal servings because each dish is designed to be part of a seven- to ten-course tasting menu. For larger servings, use the recipes as a foundation and increase the quantities proportionally to suit the flow of your meal. Generally you will not have to increase the garnishes, jus and finishing sauces unless you are more than doubling the main ingredients.

Lumière's menu concept gives diners a wider spectrum of flavors. It's the same idea as in Chinese and Japanese cuisine, where you are served many dishes and have small tastes of each. I love to eat this way myself. It's a clean and refreshing approach to food, which means that people can sit back, enjoy their evening and walk out feeling comfortable and satisfied rather than stuffed.

The menus also allow me to play with people's expectations a bit. I'm after the Wow factor, and orchestrating layers of flavor in a number of smaller courses gives me a good chance of hitting it a few times during the meal.

< Citrus-cured sockeye salmon and potato gnocchi with balsalmic glaze (page 59)

Duo des pommes de terre

POTATO PURÉE

1¼ lbs. Yukon Gold potatoes, skins on

1 cup heavy cream, lukewarm

5 Tbsp. unsalted butter, cut in cubes

5 Tbsp. mascarpone cheese

½ tsp. sea salt

GLAZED NEW POTATOES

12 oz. assorted small new potatoes, skins on

½ tsp. sea salt

1½ cups chicken or vegetable stock
    (see page 169 or 170)

3 Tbsp. unsalted butter

1 clove garlic

1 sprig thyme

1 cup whole baby leeks cut in 2½-inch
    pieces and blanched, or white parts of
    green onions, blanched

1 Tbsp. minced chives

¾ cup veal reduction or reduced
    mushroom stock (see page 167 or 170)

2 Tbsp. unsalted butter

ABOUT THE RECIPE: This unique entrée focuses on the pure flavor of the simple potato. It is a combination of Yukon Gold potatoes whipped with mascarpone cheese and baby new potatoes roasted and glazed.

Not far north of Vancouver is the Pemberton Valley, one of the world's major seed potato areas. At Lumière, we are fortunate enough to source our potatoes from there. Organic farmers Doug and Jeanette Helmer produce wonderful varieties, such as the Dutch Binjes, Yukon Golds, Rheingolds, Roses and Pontiacs. Baby Russets or fingerling potatoes can also be used for the glazed potatoes in this recipe.

TO PREPARE POTATO PURÉE: Leaving the skin on prevents the potatoes from absorbing excess water, which would make the purée too moist. Place the potatoes in a pot, add enough salted water to cover and bring to a boil over high heat. Reduce heat and simmer until tender, 15–20 minutes. Drain.

Peel the potatoes and process through a ricer or a fine-mesh sieve set over a pot on medium-low heat. Keeping the potatoes at a consistent heat will allow them to absorb the butter and will prevent them from becoming gluey. Slowly fold half of the lukewarm cream into the potatoes then gently fold in the butter, one piece at a time. If you mix the potatoes too quickly when adding the cream or the butter, the mixture will become sticky. Pass the whipped potatoes again through a fine-mesh sieve into a separate pot. Cover tightly, set aside and keep warm.

Before serving, heat the potatoes lightly. Thin the mascarpone with a bit of cream and then fold gently into the whipped potatoes. Season with salt and freshly ground white pepper. Fold in as much of the remaining cream as you need to reach desired consistency.

GLAZED NEW POTATOES: Preheat oven to 375° F. Place the potatoes, salt, stock, butter, garlic and thyme in a large casserole. Cover and transfer to the preheated oven. Bake until the potatoes are tender.

Remove the potatoes from the casserole and set aside, keeping them warm. Strain the liquid into a large nonstick pan over medium-high heat and reduce until syrupy. Increase the heat to high and add the potatoes to the pan; continue to cook the potatoes with the reduced liquid, shaking frequently, until the potatoes are well coated with the glaze. Add baby leeks and heat for a further minute to warm and glaze. Add the chives and season with salt and freshly ground white pepper.

Bring the veal reduction to a boil and reduce by half. Whisk in the butter.

TO ASSEMBLE: Place a scoop of the whipped potatoes in each of 4 soup plates, place the glazed potatoes on top or on the side of the whipped potatoes. Drizzle a portion of the reduced stock around the potatoes. Serve immediately.

WINE: An elegant Pinot Noir.

Serves 4 · photo, page 24

*Spring vegetable ragout with wild
mushroom consommé (facing)*

Spring vegetable ragout with wild mushroom consommé

CONSOMMÉ
whites of 2 large eggs
½ cup finely chopped mushroom
    trimmings and button mushrooms
3 cups mushroom stock (see page 170)

RAGOUT
8 baby artichokes, halved
juice of ½ lemon
1½ cups vegetable stock (see page 170)
½ cup white wine
4 sprigs thyme
½ tsp. sea salt
2 cloves garlic, crushed

8 whole baby carrots
16 pearl onions
12 small asparagus spears
½ lb. thin green beans
⅓ cup shelled green peas

2 tsp. unsalted butter
1 cup wild mushrooms, such as
    chanterelles or morels, trimmings
    reserved
basic gnocchi (optional, see page 173)
fresh thyme for garnish
extra virgin olive oil for garnish

ABOUT THE RECIPE: This easy dish captures spring and also reflects what the restaurant is about. Each vegetable gets to speak for itself, its flavor and color intact because of the preliminary blanching. The rich mushroom essence of the consommé enhances the pure flavor of the vegetables.

TO PREPARE CONSOMMÉ: Lightly beat egg whites until foamy. Incorporate chopped mushrooms and season with salt and white pepper. In a medium pot, stir egg white mixture into cold mushroom stock and bring to a gentle simmer over medium heat. The egg whites will cook and float to the top, forming a raft. When this happens, remove pot from heat and slowly spoon consommé into a cheesecloth-lined sieve set over a clean pot. Gently break the raft in the center and carefully ladle the liquid out through the hole. Don't get any of the raft in the consommé.

RAGOUT: To prepare the artichokes, place them in a large pot with lemon juice, vegetable stock, wine, thyme, salt and garlic. Bring to a boil, reduce heat to simmer, cover and cook until the artichokes are fork tender.

In a large pot of boiling salted water, blanch each of the remaining vegetables separately. Cook the vegetables until they're done to your preference. They will cook some more in the casserole, so leave a bit of bite. Have a bowl of ice water on the side and plunge vegetables in to stop the cooking and preserve the color. Peel the onions after blanching.

In a large saucepan, melt the butter over medium heat and sauté the mushrooms until tender. Add 2 cups of the mushroom consommé, carrots and pearl onions. Add gnocchi if using. Bring to a simmer and add artichokes, asparagus, green beans and peas.

Remove from heat. Season with salt and freshly ground white pepper and add thyme and a few drops of olive oil. Serve immediately.

WINE: A Loire Valley Cabernet Franc.

Serves 4

Goat cheese ravioli with a light curry froth

RAVIOLI

½ lb. Yukon Gold potatoes, skins on

¼ cup goat cheese

4 Tbsp. olive oil

3 Tbsp. finely chopped chives

2 Tbsp. julienned flat-leaf parsley

¼ recipe pasta dough (see page 173)

CURRY FROTH

1 Tbsp. unsalted butter

⅓ cup sliced onions

1 pear, peeled, cored and thinly sliced

2 cloves garlic, finely chopped

1 bay leaf

2 sprigs thyme

1 Tbsp. curry powder

1 tsp. ground turmeric

¼ cup chicken stock (see page 169)

½ cup heavy cream

½ tsp. lemon juice

STOCK SAUCE

1 cup vegetable or chicken stock
  (see page 170 or 169)

1 Tbsp. butter

1 tsp. olive oil

ABOUT THE RECIPE: This has always been a popular item on our vegetarian menu. We use a wonderful soft-textured goat cheese made by David Wood of Salt Spring Island Cheese. David produces some of the best goat and sheep cheeses on the West Coast.

The ravioli can be made ahead and frozen. We usually serve 3 per plate for a starter course, but this recipe will make more than that. If you serve it as a main course you will have enough for a substantial serving for 4 people.

TO PREPARE RAVIOLI: Start potatoes in cold salted water and bring to a boil. Simmer until fork tender. Drain and set aside. In a mixing bowl, stir goat cheese until smooth. Peel potatoes and pass through a ricer or grate into cheese. Combine well. Add olive oil and herbs. Season with salt and freshly ground white pepper.

To make ravioli, follow method on page 173.

CURRY FROTH: In a saucepan, melt the butter over medium heat. Add the onions, pear, garlic, bay leaf and thyme. Sweat mixture until the vegetables are soft. Stir in the curry powder, turmeric and stock. Simmer to reduce by one-third. Add cream and bring to boil. Remove bay leaf and thyme. Purée the mixture in a blender and strain. The mixture should be just thick enough to coat the back of a spoon. If too thick, add more stock. Season with salt and freshly ground white pepper and add lemon juice.

STOCK SAUCE: In a large saucepan, reduce stock over medium heat until syrupy. Whisk in butter and a touch of olive oil.

TO ASSEMBLE: Before serving, cook the ravioli in 1 gallon boiling water with ⅓ cup salt. Cook half at a time, and boil uncovered for 2–3 minutes or until al dente. Drain in a colander, but do not rinse. Keep warm. Cook remaining ravioli. Add the warm ravioli to the reduced stock and stir gently to coat. Place ravioli in 6 large warmed bowls.

Heat curry froth to a gentle simmer. With an electric mixer or handheld blender, whip to a froth. Place some of the foam on the top of the ravioli and serve immediately.

WINE: A Sauvignon Blanc.

Serves 4 to 6

Garganelli pasta with spot prawns and
a lemon and thyme butter sauce (facing)

Garganelli pasta with spot prawns and a lemon and thyme butter sauce

PASTA

2½ cups garganelli pasta

olive oil

SAUCE

¼ cup rice vinegar

¼ cup dry white wine

4 sprigs thyme, plus 2 sprigs with
    leaves removed

1 tsp. heavy cream (optional)

¼ lb. unsalted butter (½ cup)

1 tsp. lemon juice

1 tsp. fine lemon zest

PASTA GLAZE

1 cup chicken stock (see page 169)

2 Tbsp. unsalted butter

1 tomato, peeled, seeded and finely chopped

1 Tbsp. chopped chives

2 Tbsp. julienned flat-leaf parsley

1 tsp. fine lemon zest

PRAWNS

12 large prawns, peeled

1 Tbsp. grapeseed oil

1 Tbsp. unsalted butter

¼ tsp. minced garlic

1 small shallot, minced

ABOUT THE RECIPE: This dish was invented one night when I was craving some pasta, and it quickly went on the menu. The pasta is just coated rather than swimming in sauce.

TO PREPARE: In a large pot of boiling salted water, cook the pasta to al dente stage. Strain without rinsing the pasta. Toss with a small amount of olive oil. Spread on a flat baking sheet to air dry—this step allows the starch to remain on the pasta, which makes sauces cling better. You can do this ahead of time and store the pasta in resealable plastic bags.

SAUCE: In a small pot, combine vinegar, wine and the 4 sprigs thyme. Reduce to a syrupy consistency. Remove thyme sprigs. Whisk in cream—this step will prevent the sauce from separating. Remove from heat and whisk in butter a bit at a time. If sauce cools too much, return to low heat, but do not let it boil. When butter is incorporated, add lemon juice and zest along with thyme leaves to mixture. Season with salt. Keep warm.

PASTA GLAZE: In a large sauté pan over medium heat, reduce stock by half. Whisk in butter. Add the pasta and toss to warm through. Add tomato, chives, parsley and lemon zest, and season to taste with salt and freshly ground white pepper.

PRAWNS: Season prawns with salt. In a nonstick frying pan, heat the oil over medium-high heat. When the pan is lightly smoking, add the prawns and quickly sauté. When prawns are pink on one side, add butter, garlic and shallot. Turn prawns and continue sautéing until cooked through. Remove from pan and keep warm.

TO ASSEMBLE: Over low heat, add the pasta and ¼ cup of the lemon and thyme sauce to the prawn juices. Toss until thoroughly warmed. Divide among 4 large bowls. Place 3 prawns on top of the pasta. Drizzle warm sauce on top of the prawns and around the plate.

WINE: A light Mâcon Chardonnay or a New Zealand Chardonnay.

Serves 4

Napoleon of Dungeness crab with curry mayonnaise and a pineapple and celery broth

PHYLLO SQUARES
1 large phyllo sheet
2 Tbsp. melted unsalted butter

BROTH
½ pineapple, skinned
4 stalks celery
juice of 1 lime

MAYONNAISE
1 egg
1 tsp. Dijon mustard

2 tsp. red wine vinegar
3 cups vegetable oil
juice of ½ lemon
½ tsp. red curry paste

CRAB FILLING
1 lb. fresh Dungeness crabmeat
1 Granny Smith apple, peeled, cored and
    finely diced
1 stalk celery, strings removed, finely diced
¼ cup julienned basil

ABOUT THE RECIPE: I've spent a lot of time in Brittany and Normandy and later, Japan. In all of those places I learned to let fish speak for itself.

This appetizer combines the natural sweetness of our succulent West Coast Dungeness crab with just a hint of curry. The phyllo squares provide a delicate crunch while the fragrant broth balances the whole dish. Make sure that the broth is very cold when you serve the dish so that you really taste the celery and pineapple.

TO PREPARE: Preheat oven to 350° F. Put the phyllo on a baking sheet and brush with butter. Fold the sheet into 2 layers lengthwise. Cut into 8 squares. Brush with melted butter, season with salt and bake until golden brown (5–7 minutes). Cool.

BROTH: In a juicer, juice the pineapple and celery in separate containers. Place containers in freezer for 10–15 minutes. Impurities will rise to the top and can be easily skimmed off. Combine pineapple juice, celery juice and lime juice and chill.

MAYONNAISE: In a food processor or blender, combine egg, mustard and vinegar and blend. With machine still running, slowly drizzle in oil until emulsified. Add lemon juice and season with salt and freshly ground white pepper. Remove ¼ cup of the mayonnaise and stir in curry paste. Remaining mayonnaise can be refrigerated and reserved for another use.

CRAB FILLING: Remove any shell and cartilage from crabmeat. Mix crabmeat with apple, celery and 1 heaping tsp. of the curry mayonnaise, or enough to moisten and bind the mixture together. Add basil. Season with salt and freshly ground white pepper.

TO ASSEMBLE: Divide half the crabmeat and apple mixture among 4 soup plates. Cover with a square of phyllo and top with another spoonful of the crab mixture. Place another layer of phyllo on top. Spoon ¼ cup of pineapple and celery broth around the napoleon and serve immediately.

WINE: A glorious Riesling again: a light Alsace, or a German Kabinett from Mosel Saar or Ruwer.

Serves 4

Tuna tartare
with tamari vinaigrette

1 lb. sushi-grade ahi or big-eye tuna

TAMARI VINAIGRETTE

⅓ cup orange juice

⅓ cup rice vinegar

2 Tbsp. tamari

1 Tbsp. ponzu sauce (available in
    Asian stores) or 1 Tbsp. equal parts
    tamari, lemon juice and mirin

¼ cup sesame oil

1 Tbsp. fresh cilantro, finely shredded

1 tsp. toasted black sesame seeds

2 tsp. finely chopped green onion

1 tomato peeled, seeded and cut into
    ¼-inch dice

2 Tbsp. shredded nori

1 avocado

¼ lemon

1 Tbsp. tobiko (flying fish roe)
    for garnish

mixed baby greens tossed with lemon
    oil (see page 171) for garnish

cilantro oil (see page 171)
    for garnish

tamari reduction (see page 58)
    for garnish (optional)

ABOUT THE RECIPE: The clean flavor of absolutely fresh tuna loves this combination of salt, sweetness and tang. This certainly has been one of the most popular items on the tasting menus. I use ahi or the harder to find big-eye tuna because of the texture and rich color of the flesh.

TO PREPARE: Cut the tuna into a very small dice, approximately ¼ inch. Dicing the fish into small pieces is easier when the fish is chilled.

For the vinaigrette, combine orange juice, vinegar, tamari and ponzu sauce. Gradually whisk in sesame oil until emulsified. Keep refrigerated until ready to use.

In a mixing bowl, just before you are ready to serve, combine tuna, cilantro, black sesame seeds, green onion and tomato. Add 4 Tbsp. tamari vinaigrette and mix gently. Season with salt and freshly ground black pepper. Taste and adjust seasonings. Add shredded nori and keep refrigerated until ready to use. Taste again before serving and add a little lemon juice, if necessary.

Before serving, peel, seed and dice avocado. Gently mix with lemon juice.

To serve, place some avocado in the middle of plates, using a cookie cutter or round mold as a guide. Place tuna tartare on top. Sprinkle with a little tobiko. Top with mixed greens. Drizzle cilantro oil and tamari reduction around tartare and remove mold. Serve immediately.

WINE: A ripe Italian Verdicchio or, our friend, the glorious Riesling.

Serves 4

Poached wild spring salmon with baby artichokes, capers, niçoise olives and roasted red peppers

1 small red bell pepper
8 baby artichokes, halved
juice of ½ lemon
1½ cups chicken stock (see page 169)
½ cup white wine
4 sprigs thyme
½ tsp. sea salt
2 cloves garlic, crushed

SAUCE
1 cup dark chicken stock (see page 169)
1 Tbsp. capers, rinsed
1 Tbsp. niçoise olives, pitted and quartered

½ lemon, peeled, seeded and cut in
    segments
1 Tbsp. extra virgin olive oil
1 Tbsp. unsalted butter

SALMON
four 4-oz. pieces spring salmon,
    skin on, scaled
1 qt. court bouillon (see page 170)
1 cup mesclun greens, rinsed and dried
    (optional)
house vinaigrette (see page 172)
parsley oil (see page 171) for garnish

ABOUT THE RECIPE: Provençal cuisine is rustic and simple but full of passion and flavor. In this recipe I've used some of the trademark ingredients of the area, such as garlic, artichokes, peppers and olives to enhance the wonderful flavor of fresh spring salmon.

TO PREPARE THE VEGETABLES: Roast red pepper in a 350° F oven or under a broiler until skin is uniformly blackened. Allow to cool and rub off blackened skin. Seed pepper and finely dice ⅓ cup. Set aside. Reserve remaining roasted pepper for another use.

Place the artichokes in a large pot with lemon juice, stock, wine, thyme, salt, and garlic. Bring to a boil, reduce heat to simmer, cover and cook until the artichokes are fork tender. Transfer the artichokes to a nonstick pan with some of the cooking liquid. Bring to a boil until the liquid is reduced and has coated the artichokes. Set aside.

SAUCE: Over medium heat, reduce stock by half. Reduce heat to medium-low and add roasted red pepper, capers, olives and lemon. Add olive oil and butter and whisk well to emulsify. Keep warm.

SALMON: Bring the court bouillon to a gentle simmer in a deep, wide pan. Place the salmon fillets in the liquid; do not allow liquid to boil. The salmon will be cooked medium rare in 3–4 minutes. Remove from heat. Keep warm.

TO ASSEMBLE: Just before serving, toss the mesclun greens with a little house vinaigrette. Taste the caper and olive sauce for seasonings. It may not need any salt because of the capers, but it might need some lemon juice.

Rewarm the artichokes and divide among 4 serving plates. Place the salmon on top of the artichokes. Spoon the sauce over top, making sure to coat the surface of the fish. (This dish can be served in a large bowl if you prefer to have more sauce.) Top with the dressed mesclun. Drizzle parsley oil around the outside of the plate. Serve immediately.

WINE: A proper southern French rosé.

Serves 4

Poached wild spring salmon with baby artichokes,
capers, niçoise olives and roasted red peppers (facing)

Braised halibut casserole with wild mushrooms and black truffle butter

TRUFFLE BUTTER
1 whole black truffle, about the size
    of a quarter
½ lb. unsalted butter, room temperature
    (1 cup)
1 tsp. fresh lemon juice

CASSEROLE
4 small artichokes
juice of ½ lemon
1½ cups vegetable stock (see page 170)
½ cup white wine
4 sprigs thyme

½ tsp. sea salt
2 cloves garlic, crushed
1 Tbsp. olive oil
1 cup wild mushrooms, such as
    chanterelles or morels, cleaned
1 clove garlic, minced
1 cup dark chicken stock (see page 169)
⅓ cup pearl onions, blanched and skinned

HALIBUT
four 3-oz. halibut fillets, skinless
2 Tbsp. olive oil

ABOUT THE RECIPE: This simple but elegant dish reads springtime all over, with wild mushrooms, pearl onions and artichokes enhancing one of the most versatile of all fish, halibut. The halibut becomes infused with all the other flavors as they cook together in the casserole.

This recipe can be made year round by substituting different kinds of mushrooms and vegetables depending on when halibut is in season. And if you don't have a truffle for the butter, use some truffle oil.

TO PREPARE TRUFFLE BUTTER: Shave half the truffle into thin slices and cut into very fine dice, about ⅛ inch. Incorporate truffles with the softened butter. Season to taste with salt, freshly ground white pepper and lemon juice. Place on a square of parchment and roll into a cylinder. Remove parchment and wrap tightly in plastic wrap. Keep refrigerated until ready to use. Reserve remaining truffle for another use.

CASSEROLE: To prepare the artichokes, place them in a large pot with lemon juice, stock, wine, thyme, salt and garlic. Bring to a boil, reduce heat to simmer, cover and cook until the artichokes are fork tender.

In a small saucepan, heat olive oil over medium heat. Add the mushrooms and garlic and sauté for about 1 minute. Season with salt and freshly ground white pepper. Transfer the mixture to a large casserole dish and add the stock. Over low heat, bring the liquid to a boil. Cover and simmer for 3 minutes. Remove from heat and add pearl onions and artichokes. Set aside.

HALIBUT: Preheat the oven to 350° F. Season each side of the halibut with salt and freshly ground white pepper. Heat the olive oil in a frying pan over high heat. Add the halibut fillets and sear until golden. Remove halibut from heat and place in the casserole on top of the mushrooms. Cover casserole and place in preheated oven for 3–4 minutes or until fish is cooked.

TO ASSEMBLE: Remove casserole from oven, add 2 Tbsp. of the truffle butter and let it melt into the liquid over low heat (or drizzle in some truffle oil). Season with salt and freshly ground white pepper. Serve immediately.

WINE: A big Chardonnay.

Serves 4 · photo, page 108

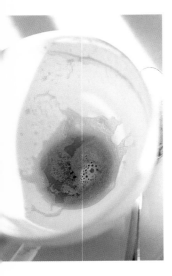

Duo des pommes de terre (page 10)

Sake and maple marinated sablefish with a citrus and soy sauce

SABLEFISH

1 cup sake

⅓ cup maple syrup

four 5-oz. portions sablefish fillets,
    skin on, scaled

SAUCE

¾ cup fresh orange juice

¼ cup fresh grapefruit juice

2 Tbsp. lime juice

¼ tsp. soy sauce

3 Tbsp. unsalted butter

2 Tbsp. chicken stock (see page 169)

1 orange, cut in segments, for garnish

1 grapefruit or lemon, cut in segments,
    for garnish

2 Tbsp. finely julienned green onions
    for garnish

2 Tbsp. finely julienned red radishes
    for garnish

1 tsp. lemon oil (see page 171) for garnish

ABOUT THE RECIPE: On a trip to Japan in February 2000, I was the guest of the Canadian Consulate and the ANA Grand Court Hotel in Nagoya. I was the featured Canadian chef asked to do a culinary exhibition using Canadian ingredients. One of the more popular recipes that evolved from the trip was this superb fish course which uses Japanese condiments infused with good old Canadian maple syrup. The buttery richness of the sablefish is a perfect match for the marinade.

TO PREPARE SABLEFISH: Bring sake to a boil and stir in maple syrup. Let cool. Place sablefish fillets in a nonreactive deep dish or small pan; cover with cooled sake–maple syrup mixture and marinate for 24 hours.

Preheat oven to 375° F. Remove the fish from the marinade and pat dry. Line a large baking sheet with parchment. Place the fish skin-side up; bake for 10 minutes.

SAUCE: Combine citrus juices and simmer gently over medium heat until reduced by half, stirring occasionally. Refrigerate until needed.

To finish the citrus and soy sauce, combine reduced citrus juice, soy sauce and stock in a small pot and bring to a gentle boil. Stir in the butter until blended. Taste for seasoning. If sauce is too tart, add a little more butter.

TO ASSEMBLE: Divide the orange, grapefruit and lemon segments among 4 bowls. Spoon sauce over the fruit segments; place the sablefish on top skin-side up. Garnish with green onions, radishes and lemon oil and serve immediately.

WINE: A glorious Riesling: a ripe Alsatian or German Auslese, or Spätslese from Pfalz.

Serves 4

Poached free-range chicken breast with a morel and white asparagus cream

1 lb. white asparagus, cleaned and peeled,
    trimmings reserved
1 qt. chicken stock (see page 169)
4 large free-range chicken breasts,
    boneless and skinless

1 Tbsp. unsalted butter
1 shallot, thinly sliced
2 cups morels, cleaned
¼ cup dry white wine
1 cup heavy cream

ABOUT THE RECIPE: This incredible dish was inspired by one of my most memorable meals. It was late at night and I had just driven through Beaune in Burgundy, so I found a small hotel in the next city. I was lucky enough to get a free table in their restaurant. That is where, for the first time, I tasted this wonderful poached chicken with a cream sauce made of its reduced poaching liquid. So straightforward, and so delicious.

The simple poaching of the meat ensures a pure, clean flavor, and the rich and delicate sauce with white asparagus and earthy morel mushrooms enrobes the meat beautifully.

TO PREPARE ASPARAGUS: In a large pot, bring salted water to a boil. Add white asparagus and simmer 4 minutes uncovered. Remove pan from heat and set aside for 3–4 minutes, still uncovered. Drain asparagus and immediately plunge into ice water to stop the cooking.

CHICKEN: In a saucepan over medium heat, bring the stock just to a boil and season with salt. Poach the chicken breasts in the stock for 10 minutes at a gentle simmer. Remove chicken from stock and cover with foil. Reheat stock on medium heat and reduce by half.

Melt butter in a saucepan over medium heat and sweat the shallot. Add morels and cook for 2–3 minutes. Add wine and reduce by half. Add reduced stock and again reduce by half. Add cream and reduce by one-third. Season with salt and freshly ground white pepper. Cut asparagus into 1-inch pieces and add to morel and chicken stock mixture.

TO ASSEMBLE: Cut each chicken breast into 3 large slices. Place a slice of chicken breast in the center of 4 large plates. Top with a small portion of mushroom mixture and repeat for the remaining 2 chicken slices, ending with the mushroom mixture. Spoon sauce over and around plate and serve immediately.

WINE: A white Burgundy or a good Champagne.

Serves 4 · photo, page 29

Roasted rack of lamb with a casserole of spring vegetables and rosemary oil

RACK OF LAMB
1 Tbsp. grapeseed oil
2 lamb racks, frenched, chine bones cut

CASSEROLE
¾ cup chicken stock (see page 169)
12 large green beans, blanched
12 large yellow wax beans, blanched
½ cup peeled fava beans, germs
    removed, chilled in water

8 baby carrots, peeled and blanched
1 tsp. chopped rosemary leaves
1 cup veal reduction (see page 167)
2 Tbsp. unsalted butter

rosemary leaves for garnish
rosemary oil (see page 171) for garnish

ABOUT THE RECIPE: We buy delicious local lamb in season from Saltspring Island, Vancouver Island and Alberta. When none of those are available my preference is for Australian lamb.

When you're buying lamb racks, look at the rib eye and make sure that it's not too small and that it's nicely marbled, especially around the fat cap. Ask the butcher to leave a thin layer of fat on top. This layer will melt into the meat as it cooks.

The secret to tender lamb is to let it rest anywhere from 10–30 minutes after it's cooked so the muscle relaxes and reabsorbs the juice.

TO PREPARE: Preheat oven to 400° F. Heat grapeseed oil in a large nonstick skillet over medium-high heat. Sear lamb racks for approximately 3 minutes. Drain any fat from the pan. Roast the lamb for 15–20 minutes, or until the internal temperature reaches 125° F for rare or 130° F for medium-rare. Remove from the oven and let rest for 5 minutes.

While the lamb is cooking, in a casserole dish combine the stock, green and yellow beans, fava beans, carrots, salt and freshly ground white pepper. Cover and bring to a boil. Drain vegetables, reserving stock in a small saucepan. Keep vegetables warm.

To stock, add rosemary leaves and veal reduction. Reduce stock by one-third. Remove from heat and strain out rosemary leaves. Return to pot and whisk in butter. Taste for seasoning. Return vegetables to sauce to warm through.

TO ASSEMBLE: Carve lamb racks into individual chops. Divide the vegetables among 4 large serving plates. Place the lamb over the vegetables. Spoon the sauce over the lamb, garnish with rosemary around the outside and drizzle with a few drops of the rosemary oil.

WINE: A big-ass Rhône red.

Serves 4

Seared foie gras with sundried tomato chutney

SUNDRIED TOMATO CHUTNEY
¼ cup sundried tomatoes, rehydrated
    and finely chopped
2 Tbsp. finely chopped niçoise olives
1 Tbsp. sherry vinegar
2 Tbsp. lemon oil (see page 171)

FOIE GRAS
1 Grade-A foie gras (approx. 1 lb.)
fleur de sel or coarse sea salt

balsamic glaze (see page 172)
    for garnish

ABOUT THE RECIPE: At the restaurant we are fortunate to use 25-year-old aged balsamic vinegar as an accent. It is very expensive and difficult to find, so I've substituted it in this recipe with a balsamic reduction glaze.

TO PREPARE CHUTNEY: In a bowl, mix the sundried tomatoes, olives, vinegar and 2 Tbsp. of the lemon oil. Cover and refrigerate the chutney overnight.

FOIE GRAS: Slice the foie gras into 8 approximately equal slices, each about 1 inch thick. Place the slices on a large plastic-wrapped plate. Score slices in a crisscross pattern on one side. Season with sea salt and freshly ground white pepper on both sides.

To sear, use two 8-inch nonstick frying pans on the stove on high heat (you never want to crowd a pan when roasting or cooking anything). When the pans start smoking lightly, remove from heat. Carefully place 4 pieces in each pan, scored-side down, and sear for approximately 1½ minutes. Pour off fat. Turn over and cook for 1½ minutes on the other side. (Since foie gras has a high fat content, it has a tendency to burn so the cooking time may be shorter depending on the bottom thickness of the pan.) Remove from heat and put foie gras on a paper towel–lined baking sheet to absorb excess fat. Season with coarse sea salt and cracked black pepper.

TO ASSEMBLE: Place 1 portion of foie gras slightly off-center on a large plate. Beside it, place the sundried tomato chutney. Drizzle balsamic glaze around the plate and serve immediately.

WINE: A Barbara Cartland wine: sticky, sweet and white—a Sauternes or late-harvest Riesling.

Serves 8

Poached free-range chicken breast with a
morel and white asparagus cream (page 26)

Brillat-Savarin cheese with strawberries and balsamic glaze

1 cup quartered strawberries
½ tsp. granulated sugar
½ tsp. fresh lemon juice
1 Tbsp. balsamic glaze (see page 172)
four 1-oz. portions Brillat-Savarin cheese

ABOUT THE RECIPE: Brillat-Savarin, from Normandy, is mild in flavor, but one of the richest cheeses you can find.

TO PREPARE: Place strawberries in small pot on low heat with sugar and lemon juice. When strawberries are warmed through, pour any liquid into another small pot. Cover strawberries and keep warm. Reduce strawberry liquid to a syrup and add balsamic glaze. Stir to warm through.

   To serve, place a small mound of strawberries next to cheese on 4 plates. Drizzle liquid over strawberries.

WINE: A big red Bordeaux or Merlot.

Serves 4

Valençay cheese with
a warm beet salad

8 baby beets
½ cup red wine
¾ cup balsamic vinegar
four 1-oz. portions Valençay cheese

ABOUT THE RECIPE: Beets and goat cheese are a classic combination. The sweetness and earthiness of beets are balanced by the tang of goat cheese.

Valençay was originally made in a pyramid shape, but Napoleon visited the region on his way home from an unsuccessful campaign in Egypt and, still being a little touchy, whacked off the top of one with his sword. You don't want to mess with a guy like that, so to this day, Valençay cheese looks like a pyramid with the top sliced off.

TO PREPARE: Trim off beet greens, leaving about ½ inch of stem attached. In a large pot, cover beets with water. Bring to a boil and continue boiling until beets are half-cooked. Remove from water and allow to cool.

Trim off ends of beets and peel. Set 4 beets aside and slice the rest into ¼-inch rounds. Place beet slices in another pot and cover with wine and ½ cup of the vinegar. Cover pot and bring to boil over medium heat. Reduce to a simmer and cook for 3–5 minutes. Remove from heat and allow to cool without taking off lid. When a knife can easily pierce the slices, remove from liquid. Reserve poaching liquid.

Finely chop the remaining 4 beets and place in a small saucepan with enough of the poaching liquid to cover. Boil until beets are soft enough to purée.

Purée chopped beets and liquid in a blender and press through a fine-mesh sieve. Stir in remaining ¼ cup of the vinegar.

To serve, warm the beet slices in a microwave for about 10 seconds. Arrange on serving plates and drizzle a small amount of the red beet reduction over. Place the cheese beside the beets and serve immediately.

WINE: A Sauvignon Blanc, or a Beaujolais Commune if you want a red.

Serves 4

Le Coutances cheese with a
mixed apple napoleon (facing)

Le Coutances cheese
with a mixed apple napoleon

POACHED APPLE

½ cup white wine

¼ cup simple syrup (see page 175)

1 sprig rosemary, finely chopped

juice of 1 lemon

1 large Fuji apple, peeled, cored and diced

four 1-oz. portions Le Coutances cheese

APPLE CHIPS

2 small Gala apples, whole

½ cup simple syrup (see page 175)

¼ cup water

juice of 1 lemon

¼ tsp. ground allspice

ABOUT THE RECIPE: Le Coutances cheese comes from Normandy. Made from unpasteurized cow's milk and matured briefly over four to six weeks, it is attractively marketed in small round wooden boxes.

TO PREPARE POACHED APPLE: In a saucepan, combine the wine, syrup, rosemary and lemon juice and warm over medium heat to a simmer. Add the diced apples and remove from heat. Cover and allow to sit 3–5 minutes, or until apples are tender. Strain, cool and refrigerate. The poaching liquid can be refrigerated and used for another purpose.

APPLE CHIPS: Preheat oven to 250° F. Using a mandoline or a sharp knife, cut the apples into paper thin rounds, removing seeds as they appear. In a saucepan, combine the syrup, water and lemon juice and bring to a boil. Remove from heat and add the apple slices. When the apples are transparent, remove carefully with a slotted spoon and transfer onto a parchment-lined baking sheet. Sprinkle the apple with allspice.

Bake for 25–45 minutes, or until the apples are dry. Remove from baking sheet and place on a cooling rack. Store in an airtight container.

TO ASSEMBLE: To serve, place an apple chip on a serving plate, add a small amount of the diced apples and top with another chip. Repeat. Serve cheese next to the apple napoleon.

WINE: An off-dry Loire Chenin Blanc.

Serves 4

Chocolate tango cake with bittersweet chocolate sorbet

CHOCOLATE SORBET

1 cup granulated sugar

3½ cups water

2 oz. bittersweet Valrhona chocolate,
    roughly chopped

1 cup cocoa powder

ALMOND PRALINE

1 cup granulated sugar

1 cup sliced almonds

5 Tbsp. unsalted butter

TANGERINE CAKE

8 Tbsp. unsalted butter

¼ cup granulated sugar

pulp of ½ vanilla bean

zest and juice of 1 tangerine

2 egg yolks

¼ cup ground almonds

¼ cup all-purpose flour

¼ tsp. baking powder

3 Tbsp. Essensia

CHOCOLATE CAKE

¼ lb. unsalted butter (½ cup)

4 oz. bittersweet Valrhona chocolate

2 eggs

2 egg yolks

¼ cup granulated sugar

2 tsp. all-purpose flour

TANGERINE SYRUP

juice of 2 tangerines

juice of ½ lemon

3 Tbsp. Essensia

2 tsp. granulated sugar

TANGERINE JUS

zest of 1 tangerine

juice of 4 tangerines

juice of 1 lemon

pulp of ½ vanilla bean

2 Tbsp. granulated sugar

1 tsp. cornstarch

ABOUT THE RECIPE: I created this dessert with Rhonda Viani, my pastry chef at the time, for the 1999 Quady Dessert Competition. The object was to match a dessert to Quady's orange muscat dessert wine, Essensia. This matches perfectly, and it won the competition.

TO PREPARE CHOCOLATE SORBET: In a saucepan, combine sugar and water and bring to a boil. Place chocolate in a heatproof bowl and pour in the hot sugar water, whisking until chocolate is melted. Whisk in cocoa powder. Allow mixture to cool to room temperature. Freeze according to instructions on page 175.

ALMOND PRALINE: In a small, heavy-bottomed pot, melt the sugar over medium-low heat, increase heat to medium and boil until golden brown. Stir in almonds and butter. Spread mixture thinly on a parchment-lined baking sheet. Cover with another layer of parchment and cool.

TANGERINE CAKE: Cream together butter, sugar, vanilla and tangerine zest until fluffy. Beat in egg yolks one at a time. In a separate bowl, combine ground almonds, flour and baking powder. Add to wet ingredients alternately with combined tangerine juice and Essensia.

CHOCOLATE CAKE: Melt butter and chocolate together in a double boiler over simmering water. Remove from heat.

In a bowl over hot water, beat eggs, yolks and sugar until whisk leaves a thin trail when pulled through. Temper egg mixture with ¼ cup of the melted chocolate. Fold tempered egg mixture into chocolate. Sift in flour and incorporate well. Cover and refrigerate for 10 minutes.

Preheat oven to 325° F. Butter and flour twelve 2-inch metal molds or 3-inch ramekins and place on a greased baking sheet. Fill halfway with tangerine cake batter. Using a large tip, pipe chocolate cake batter into center of each mold, starting at the bottom and piping upwards, until molds are three-quarters full. Bake for 10 minutes or until slightly springy to touch. Remove cakes from oven and unmold. While cakes are still hot from the oven, soak generously with hot tangerine syrup.

TANGERINE SYRUP: While cakes are baking, combine tangerine and lemon juices, Essensia and sugar in a small pot over medium heat and bring to a boil.

TANGERINE JUS: Combine tangerine zest and juice, lemon juice, vanilla, sugar and cornstarch in a small pot and bring to a boil over medium-high heat. Boil briefly until jus is clear and thickened.

TO ASSEMBLE: Place cakes off-center on 4 large plates. Drizzle tangerine jus around cakes. Crush about ¼ cup of praline with a rolling pin. Place a small mound of crushed praline beside each cake. Place a scoop of sorbet on crushed praline and top with a larger piece of praline.

WINE: Essensia makes sense, or a Banyuls.

Serves 12

*Lemon and buttermilk panna cotta
with a blueberry compote (facing)*

Lemon and buttermilk panna cotta
with a blueberry compote

LEMON LAYER

2 Tbsp. gelatin

¼ cup cold water

¼ cup + 2 Tbsp. simple syrup
    (see page 175)

¼ cup + 2 Tbsp. lemon juice

BUTTERMILK LAYER

1 Tbsp. gelatin

⅓ cup cold water

1 cup heavy cream

¼ cup sugar

1½ cups buttermilk

BLUEBERRY COMPOTE

⅓ cup simple syrup (see page 175)

1½ cups fresh or frozen blueberries

1 Tbsp. lemon juice

CANDIED ZEST

zest of ½ lemon, cut in thin strips

zest of ½ lime, cut in thin strips

¼ cup water

⅛ cup sugar

ABOUT THE RECIPE: This is a beautiful two-layer panna cotta with a translucent lemon layer that crowns the silky buttermilk bottom. Light and velvety and smooth, it is based upon the Italian dessert translated as "cooked cream." Although it has a custardlike texture, there are no eggs in this dessert.

TO PREPARE LEMON LAYER: Sprinkle gelatin over ¼ cup cold water and let gelatin absorb all the water, 1–2 minutes. Place gelatin and simple syrup in a small saucepan and stir over low heat until the gelatin is dissolved. Pour the lemon juice into a small mixing bowl. Add the dissolved gelatin and stir well to mix. Pour into ½-cup ramekins and refrigerate until set.

BUTTERMILK LAYER: Sprinkle the gelatin over ⅓ cup cold water. Let the gelatin absorb all the water, about 2 minutes. Place gelatin, cream and sugar in a saucepan over low heat and stir until the gelatin and sugar have dissolved. Stir in buttermilk. Pour into the ramekins over the lemon gelatin and refrigerate until set.

BLUEBERRY COMPOTE: In a saucepan over medium heat, warm up syrup. Remove from heat and stir in 1 cup of the blueberries. Allow to sit for 2–3 minutes. Transfer mixture to a blender, process and strain through a fine-mesh sieve. Add lemon juice and the remaining blueberries to the blueberry sauce.

CANDIED ZEST: Cover zest strips with cold water in a small pot. Bring to a boil and drain. Repeat two more times. Add ¼ cup water and the sugar. Boil gently until the zest is opaque and most of the syrup is absorbed. Transfer to a plate to cool.

TO ASSEMBLE: Run a knife around the panna cottas and press lightly on the surface. This will break the seal and make it easier to unmold onto a serving plate. Spoon some of the compote around each panna cotta and top with candied zest. Serve immediately.

WINE: Once again, the lovely Moscato d'Asti.

Serves 6 to 8

Lime curd Pavlova with a coconut citrus sauce

CARDAMOM-INFUSED WHIPPED CREAM
½ cup heavy cream
2 cardamom pods, crushed
zest of ½ tangelo or tangerine

MERINGUE
4 large egg whites
1 cup berry sugar
½ tsp. white wine vinegar
1 tsp. cornstarch, sifted

LIME CURD
¼ lb. unsalted butter (½ cup)
¼ cup heavy cream

3 large eggs
2 large egg yolks
¾ cup lime juice
¾ cup sugar

COCONUT CITRUS SAUCE
½ cup coconut milk
zest and juice of ½ tangelo or tangerine
1 Tbsp. brown sugar
2 cardamom pods, crushed

1 banana for garnish

ABOUT THE RECIPE: When my pastry chef Rhonda Viani was about to leave for Australia, we got excited about doing something to send her off, so we did a take on Australia's favorite dessert. Everything in this recipe can be done ahead, leaving just the assembly to do before serving.

TO PREPARE WHIPPED CREAM: Combine cream, cardamom pods and citrus zest in a heavy saucepan and heat over medium-high heat just to a boil. Remove, cool, cover and refrigerate overnight to infuse. Strain through a fine-mesh sieve. Transfer infused cream to a chilled mixing bowl and whip until stiff. Refrigerate in an airtight container.

MERINGUE: Preheat oven to 250° F. In a large clean stainless steel bowl, beat the egg whites until stiff while gradually adding the sugar. Add the vinegar and whip until well incorporated. Gently fold in sifted cornstarch.

Attach a ½-inch plain tip to a large piping bag and pipe large spiral peaks (3–4 inches across) onto a parchment-lined baking sheet. Bake until crisp, 1–2 hours. Cool to room temperature. Meringues can be kept in an airtight container at room temperature until needed.

LIME CURD: In a double boiler over simmering water, combine the butter and cream. In a mixing bowl, beat together the eggs and yolks. Temper by gradually stirring in ¼ cup of the warm cream. Stir egg mixture into remaining cream in the double boiler. In a small bowl, combine lime juice and sugar. Stir into egg mixture. Stir constantly until the lime curd thickens and coats the back of the spoon. Do not allow it to overcook or it will curdle.

SAUCE: Combine coconut milk, citrus juice and zest, sugar and cardamom pods in a heavy saucepan and heat over medium-high heat just to a boil. Reduce heat and simmer for 10 minutes. Strain.

TO ASSEMBLE: Before serving, bring coconut citrus sauce to a simmer over medium heat. Cut banana into ½-inch slices and add to hot coconut citrus sauce until banana is soft; remove from heat and allow to cool for 5 minutes.

Place a meringue in the center of a serving plate and top with a large spoonful of lime curd. Cover the curd with some cooked banana pieces. Drizzle with some of the coconut citrus sauce and a spoonful of the whipped cardamom-infused whipped cream. Serve immediately.

WINE: A Canadian Riesling icewine.

Serves 4 to 6

{ S U M M E R }

SUMMER FOR ME is a place: the hot, dry, incredibly fertile Okanagan Valley. In summer,

hundreds of roadside stands are loaded with peaches, cherries, apricots, pears and plums,

corn, peas, cucumbers, tomatoes—some of the best produce in the world. My mother was

born in the Okanagan and my aunt owned a cherry orchard, so we spent a month there

every year when I was growing up. In my mind, the freedom of running around barefoot in

swim trunks all day is linked with the unadorned flavors of absolutely fresh, sun-warmed

fruit and vegetables. Mom would buy corn and tomatoes; and there, without too much

more fuss, was dinner. After our holiday we'd return to Vancouver with a trunk full of fruit

for pies and preserves, and I remember how just opening a jar of home-canned peaches

could brighten a wet winter day. Now, in the food at Lumière I try to recapture something

of the freedom and exuberance of a kid's Okanagan summer.

Summer

VEGETARIAN MENU

Heirloom tomato gazpacho with
Dijon mustard ice cream   *50*

Haricot vert salad with lemon and
thyme crème fraîche   *45*

Mushroom ragout with oven-dried
tomatoes and chickpea fritters   *46*

Garganelli pasta with summer truffles,
artichokes and lemon butter   *54*

Reblochon cheese with
kumquat marmalade   *74*

Apricot sorbet with an apricot
and lime jus   *175, 178*

Lemon and basil tart with
lemon sorbet   *75*

Alsace tarte flambée   *55*

Carpaccio of ahi tuna with a frozen
shiso and celery vinaigrette   *58*

Foie gras torchon with vanilla brioche
and wine-poached peaches   *70*

Seared scallops with green pea ravioli and
a summer truffle butter sauce   *53*

Roasted poussin in a soy, icewine and
mustard sauce with a potato pavé   *66*

Seared halibut in a warm
herb vinaigrette   *63*

Herb-crusted beef tenderloin
with chanterelles and a shallot and
caper jus   *69*

Coulommiers cheese with a watercress
and watermelon salad   *72*

Blueberry sorbet with lemon
and tarragon jus   *175, 179*

Goat cheesecake in a praline crust
with cherry port sauce   *78*

SEAFOOD MENU

Chilled cucumber and watermelon soup
with Dungeness crab   *51*

Citrus-cured sockeye salmon and potato
gnocchi with balsamic glaze   *59*

Scallop carpaccio with jalapeño,
mint and cilantro   *57*

Seared Pacific cod with a fricassé of
mussels, clams and chorizo with
parsley oil   *60*

Brie de Meaux cheese with
candied tomatoes   *72*

Watermelon and kaffir lime granité   *177*

Orange bavarois with mango sauce   *77*

Haricot vert salad with lemon and
thyme crème fraîche (facing)

Haricot vert salad with lemon and thyme crème fraîche

¼ lb. haricots verts or thin fresh
    green beans
¼ lb. thin wax beans
fine zest of 1 lemon

juice of ½ lemon
1 cup crème fraîche
1 Tbsp. fresh thyme leaves
lemon oil (see page 171) for garnish

ABOUT THE RECIPE: This is another wonderful idea that one of my sous-chefs, Marnie Coldham, came up with. I asked her to do something with haricots verts that we could put on the vegetarian menu and she devised this astonishingly refreshing salad.

The true French haricot vert is finer and thinner than the larger North American beans. Look for the tiniest, thinnest, most delicate beans you can find.

TO PREPARE: Bring a pot of salted water to a boil. Add the beans and cook until al dente, 2–3 minutes depending on the size. Do not overcook, as you want to retain the bright color. When they're ready, drain and immediately immerse the beans in ice water. Remove and drain well.

Combine the lemon zest, lemon juice, crème fraîche and thyme. Season with salt and freshly ground white pepper and set aside.

To serve the salad, cut beans in half diagonally and place in a large bowl. Toss with the lemon and thyme crème fraîche. Season to taste with fleur de sel and freshly ground white pepper. Drizzle with lemon oil.

WINE: A crisp Sancerre or Pouilly-Fumé; a New Zealand Sauvignon Blanc works a treat too.

Serves 4

Mushroom ragout with oven-dried tomatoes and chickpea fritters

FRITTERS

5 Tbsp. olive oil

4 cups vegetable stock (see page 170)

2 cups chickpea flour

1 tsp. minced garlic

zest of 1 lemon

RAGOUT

1 Tbsp. unsalted butter

¾ lb. assorted wild mushrooms,
    trimmed and cleaned

½ tsp. minced garlic

1 Tbsp. thyme leaves

OVEN-DRIED TOMATOES

4 roma tomatoes

4 Tbsp. extra virgin olive oil

2 cloves garlic

3 sprigs thyme, stems removed

¼ cup balsamic glaze (see page 172),
    for garnish

mesclun greens for garnish

ABOUT THE RECIPE: This recipe is perfect to make when tomatoes are in season in late summer. I prefer meatier tomatoes such as romas. These aren't dried right out, just concentrated a bit. They're really versatile—good to add to sauces, pastas and salads.

The chickpea fritters make an interesting alternative to french fries. They work well with mushrooms in the vegetarian menus and they're fabulous with meat. If you're ever looking for a unique starch component to your meal, try them.

TO PREPARE FRITTERS: Line a baking sheet with parchment paper or plastic wrap and brush with 1 Tbsp. of the olive oil. In a medium bowl, mix stock, flour and remaining 4 Tbsp. olive oil. Press mixture through a sieve into a heavy-bottomed pot.

Add minced garlic to chickpea batter and season with salt and freshly ground white pepper. Cook over medium heat, stirring constantly until the mixture is thickened. Add zest and stir. Pour mixture onto prepared pan and spread to a thickness of about ½ inch. Allow to cool, and refrigerate for 2–3 hours.

Preheat deep fryer to 350° F. Cut chickpea mixture into desired shapes and deep-fry until golden brown.

RAGOUT: In a large nonstick frying pan over medium-high heat, melt butter and sauté mushrooms. Add garlic and finish cooking mushrooms to golden brown. Remove from heat and toss with thyme leaves. Season with salt and freshly ground white pepper. Keep warm.

OVEN-DRIED TOMATOES: Blanch tomatoes for 20 seconds in boiling water. Immediately plunge into ice water. Remove peels and cores, cut in half from core end to bottom and hollow out each half.

Preheat oven to 250° F. Combine oil, garlic and thyme in a bowl and toss to coat tomatoes. Place the tomatoes cut-side down on a baking sheet and roast for 1–2 hours. Remove tomatoes and allow to cool. They can be refrigerated in an airtight container for up to a week.

TO ASSEMBLE: Warm the balsamic reduction in a small pot. Portion mushroom ragout among 4 plates. Place 2 tomato pieces on mushrooms and top with a chickpea fritter. Place a small mound of greens on fritter. Drizzle balsamic glaze around the mushrooms and serve immediately.

WINE: A Cabernet Franc or Chianti.

Serves 4

Crème fraîche

This staple of French cuisine is a cultured cream. Its tangy flavor
and silky smoothness make it useful in both sweet and savory dishes.
Most specialty food stores carry crème fraîche, but you can make
a good substitute by combining 1 cup cream with ⅓ cup buttermilk
and 1 tsp. lemon juice in a glass container. (The standard propor-
tions are 3 parts cream to 1 part buttermilk, plus a little lemon juice.)
Cover and let stand at room temperature in a warm place for 8 to
24 hours, or until very thick. Give it a shake every hour or so to
keep it from breaking up. Stir well before covering, and refrigerate
up to a week. Crème fraîche is an ideal addition for sauces or soups,
but it must be put in at the last moment and should not be boiled.
It's a great accompaniment to fresh fruit and desserts in place of
whipped cream.

< *Chilled purée of English pea soup with*
crème fraîche and caviar (page 6)

Heirloom tomato gazpacho with Dijon mustard ice cream

GAZPACHO

1 cup coarsely chopped red onions

1 cup coarsely chopped red bell peppers

1 cup English cucumber, cut into
    1-inch chunks

1 cup peeled and chopped red
    heirloom tomatoes

1½ tsp. minced garlic

¼ tsp. cayenne

1 Tbsp. white wine vinegar

½ cup extra virgin olive oil

1 Tbsp. fresh lemon juice

2 cups fresh tomato juice

1 sprig thyme

ICE CREAM

2 cups heavy cream

⅔ cup Dijon mustard

6 large egg yolks

extra virgin olive oil for garnish

ABOUT THE RECIPE: Gazpacho is a wonderful, cooling summertime soup. Fresh, ripe homegrown tomatoes give it the flavor; the mustard ice cream gives it a twist.

I enjoy experimenting with the subtly different tastes of the old tomato varieties that are being revived by farmers in B.C.'s Okanagan Valley.

TO PREPARE GAZPACHO: Combine all gazpacho ingredients in a food processor and blend to desired consistency. For a very fine soup, purée until smooth and strain through a fine-mesh sieve. This makes approximately 2 quarts. Refrigerate in an airtight container until ready to serve.

ICE CREAM: Mix the cream and mustard in a saucepan and bring to a boil. Remove from the heat, cover and allow to infuse for 10 minutes.

Place the yolks in a medium bowl and whisk until they are slightly thickened. Continue to whisk, and drizzle in half of the warm cream-and-mustard mixture. Return this to the remaining cream-and-mustard mixture in the saucepan and whisk to combine.

Place the saucepan over medium heat and cook, stirring continually with a wooden spoon until the mixture thickens slightly or reaches 175° F. Do not allow the mixture to boil as it will separate. Remove the pan from the heat and immediately strain the custard through a fine-mesh sieve into a bowl.

Set the bowl of custard in a larger bowl of ice water and stir occasionally until custard is cold. For smoother ice cream, cover the custard and refrigerate for up to 1 day.

Pour the custard into the ice cream maker and freeze for approximately 10–15 minutes. Serve immediately, or freeze in an airtight container for up to 3 days.

TO ASSEMBLE: To serve, place a scoop of the mustard ice cream in each of 4 bowls. Season the chilled gazpacho with salt and freshly ground white pepper and ladle it around the ice cream. Serve immediately. As a garnish, drizzle some extra virgin olive oil on top of the gazpacho.

WINE: A light Chianti or, for white, Grüner Veltliner from Austria.

Serves 4

Chilled cucumber and watermelon soup
with Dungeness crab

2 large field cucumbers, peeled and seeded

1 tsp. sea salt

1½ cups watermelon

1½-inch piece English cucumber,
    peeled and seeded

1 thin slice cantaloupe, peeled
    and seeded

¼ avocado (optional)

¼ cup diced, seeded watermelon
    (¼-inch dice)

½ cup Dungeness crabmeat or
    meat of 8 crab legs

4 tsp. fresh dill

1 tsp. lemon juice

4 tsp. dill oil (see page 171)
    for garnish

ABOUT THE RECIPE: Cucumber juice makes a brilliant and refreshing soup. The cucumber water is delicate yet it has a wonderful taste and an aroma of freshness. The sweetness of the watermelon balances the slight bitterness of the cucumber.

This recipe was inspired by a dish I once had at Charlie Trotter's restaurant in Chicago. I've added our local Dungeness crab because I love crabmeat with broths, and this uncooked "broth" takes that combination one more step.

TO PREPARE: Chill 4 soup bowls. It is very important that the bowls be ice cold. Cold brings out the vibrancy and flavor of the soup.

Use either a juicer or a strainer to make field cucumber and watermelon waters. If using a juicer, juice the field cucumbers and add salt. Clean the juicer and juice the 1½ cups watermelon into a separate container. Place both containers in the refrigerator. After 10 minutes, any impurities will float to the top and can be removed.

Or, if straining the juices, cut field cucumbers into chunks and purée until smooth in food processor or blender. Add salt. Transfer the purée to a cheesecloth-lined strainer set over a bowl. Press the purée with the back of a spoon to release juice. Discard remaining purée.

Place the 1½ cups watermelon in a clean cheesecloth-lined strainer and press out the juice into a separate bowl. Discard remaining purée. Cover both juices and refrigerate. Remove any impurities that float to the top.

TO ASSEMBLE: Cut English cucumber, cantaloupe and avocado into ¼-inch dice. Combine with diced watermelon and divide among 4 bowls. Add crabmeat and sprinkle with fresh dill. Mix the chilled watermelon water, cucumber water and lemon juice. Taste for seasonings. You might need a little salt and more lemon juice. Pour over the diced fruit. Drizzle with dill oil and sprinkle on some freshly cracked white pepper.

WINE: A nice dry or off-dry Chenin Blanc, or a richer style Semillon; Chardonnay, if you must.

Serves 4 · photo, page 64

Seared scallops with green pea ravioli
and a summer truffle butter sauce (facing)

Seared scallops with green pea ravioli and a summer truffle butter sauce

RAVIOLI

½ lb. shelled fresh green peas

4 oz. mascarpone cheese (½ cup)

4 oz. ricotta cheese, drained (½ cup)

¼ lb. unsalted butter, room temperature
     (½ cup)

¼ recipe pasta dough (see page 173)

SAUCE

⅓ cup rice vinegar

⅛ cup dry white wine

1 tsp. heavy cream (optional)

⅓ cup unsalted butter, chilled and cubed

1 Tbsp. finely chopped black summer
     truffles

¼ tsp. truffle oil

1 Tbsp. lemon juice

4 large scallops, tendon removed

1 Tbsp. grapeseed oil

finely shaved black truffles for garnish
     (optional)

ABOUT THE RECIPE: This is a signature dish that pops up in the spring and summer because it's light, yet so intensely flavored. This dish went over really well when we served it in June 2000 at James Beard House in New York.

TO PREPARE RAVIOLI: Blanch peas in salted boiling water for 1 minute. Plunge peas into ice water and drain. Purée in a food processor. Blend in the mascarpone, ricotta and butter and mix well. Season to taste. Cover and refrigerate for 15 minutes. Make pasta dough and fill according to directions on page 173.

   SAUCE: To prepare the butter sauce, simmer the vinegar and wine over medium heat and reduce until it forms a light syrup. If inexperienced at making butter sauces, you can prevent the sauce from breaking by adding the cream at this stage. Reduce the heat to low and whisk in butter, one piece at a time, until well incorporated. Add truffles and/or truffle oil, lemon juice and salt. Set aside and keep warm. Be careful not to bring it to a boil.

TO ASSEMBLE: Add the ravioli to a pot of salted boiling water. Cook for 3–4 minutes, or until pasta is al dente. Drain. Ravioli can be reheated at serving time by dipping in boiling water for 10 seconds.

   Season scallops on both sides with salt and freshly ground white pepper. Heat the grapeseed oil in a nonstick frying pan over medium-high heat. When hot, sear scallops 1½ minutes on each side; set aside and let rest for 2 minutes. Any juices that come from the scallops can be added to the butter sauce.

   To serve, place a scallop in a serving dish and top with one of the ravioli. Drizzle with warm butter sauce and garnish with sliced truffles.

WINE: A rich Bordeaux, Mersault or big New World Chardonnay.

Serves 4

Garganelli pasta with summer truffles, artichokes and lemon butter

1 cup chicken stock (see page 169)

4 Tbsp. unsalted butter

1 Tbsp. lemon juice

3 cups garganelli pasta

1 cup baby artichokes, halved

¼ cup fresh peas

one 2-oz. jar black truffles, juice reserved
   or one summer truffle, finely diced

2 Tbsp. grated Parmesan cheese

ABOUT THE RECIPE: This is one of the best dishes in this entire book. It truly reflects my philosophy that food should be light and simple. It is easy to prepare but stunning in flavor when done properly. Be careful not to add too much butter at the end—add just enough to coat. Don't drown the pasta in the sauce either. It's best when the sauce just coats the pasta. The truffles elevate the dish, but it will be wonderful even if you leave them out.

TO PREPARE: To make the sauce, reduce stock by two-thirds or until syrupy in a large saucepan over high heat. Whisk in butter and add lemon juice; set aside.

In a large pot of boiling salted water, cook the pasta to al dente stage. Strain without rinsing the pasta. Toss with a small amount of olive oil. Spread on a flat baking sheet to air dry—this step allows the starch to remain on the pasta, which makes sauces cling better. You can do this ahead of time and store the pasta in resealable plastic bags.

In another pot of boiling, salted water, blanch the halved artichokes and the peas separately until just tender. Drain and set aside.

Reheat the sauce over low heat and add the diced truffles and any reserved juice. Add the peas and artichokes. Add the pasta and toss to coat with the sauce. Season with salt and freshly ground white pepper and garnish with Parmesan cheese.

WINE: A rich white Méritage or Bordeaux.

Serves 4

Alsace tarte flambée

8–10 oz. fresh puff pastry dough or
   1 package frozen puff pastry, thawed
⅔ cup fromage blanc or Quark cheese
3 Tbsp. heavy cream

2 egg yolks
pinch of nutmeg
3 strips bacon, cut into thin strips
½ medium onion, finely chopped

ABOUT THE RECIPE: In Alsace, when you want to sit back with friends and have a beer or a Pinot Gris, you'll probably order this Alsatian version of pizza as well. It's a great way to start a meal. At Johnny Letzer's Maison Letzer north of Strasbourg they do nothing but tarte flambée. One of my mentors, Michel Jacob, did much of his training in Johnny Letzer's kitchen. I was privileged to spend a weekend there, and I learned how to make this Alsace specialty.

The flambée refers to the crust, which is a little bit dark on the bottom for crunch.

Many bakeries sell fresh puff pastry on special order.

TO PREPARE: On a lightly floured flat surface, roll the pastry to ⅛-inch thickness. Cut into disks about 3 inches in diameter and place on a lightly greased heavy baking sheet. Or, roll out to fit a pizza pan or pizza stone.

Mix together the fromage blanc, cream, egg yolks, nutmeg and a pinch of salt. Spread a small portion of the cheese mixture on each pastry disk. Scatter with the bacon and onion; chill or freeze on a parchment-lined tray until needed. These tarts will keep well in the freezer for two weeks if tightly covered.

Place the pizza pan or stone on the bottom rack of the oven, then heat to 450° F. When the over has reached 450° F, place the tarte on the pizza pan or stone and bake for approximately 15 minutes or until undersides are golden brown. Serve warm.

WINE: An Alsace Pinot Gris—or a beer.

Yields twelve 3-inch rounds or one 12-inch pizza

Scallop carpaccio with jalapeño,
mint and cilantro (facing)

Scallop carpaccio with jalapeño, mint and cilantro

4 very large scallops, tendon removed
1 tsp. seeded and finely minced jalapeño
    pepper
½ ripe tomato, peeled, seeded and
    cut into ¼-inch dice

1 Tbsp. finely julienned fresh mint leaves
1 Tbsp. finely julienned cilantro
6 Tbsp. extra virgin olive oil
juice of 1 lime
juice of 1 lemon

ABOUT THE RECIPE: The true master of making seafood simple is Eric Ripert of Le Bernardin in New York. Everything is about freshness, and he puts seafood on the plate without mucking with it too much. After I ate at his restaurant I had the confidence to make seafood shine.

We use the richly flavored Alaskan scallops: raw or cooked they have a lovely sweetness. With all these flavors working on the palate at the same time, this dish is intense yet light and refined. To me, it really represents how seafood should be prepared.

TO PREPARE: Cut each scallop horizontally into 4 thin slices. Place the 4 slices on a cutting board between 2 sheets of plastic wrap. Lightly pound the scallops so that they become thinner. Remove the top plastic sheet and invert the other sheet with the scallop quarters onto one of 4 serving plates. Repeat with remaining scallops. The scallops should stick to the plates. Place in the refrigerator, still covered with plastic wrap until ready to serve.

To serve, remove the plastic wrap from the plates. Combine the jalapeño, tomato, mint and cilantro and sprinkle some over each of the scallops; season with sea salt and freshly ground white pepper. Drizzle 1½ Tbsp. oil on each plate, making sure that each of the scallops is coated. Sprinkle with the lemon and lime juices and serve immediately.

WINE: A Gewürztraminer with structure, meaning probably not from California.

Serves 4

Carpaccio of ahi tuna with a
frozen shiso and celery vinaigrette

FROZEN VINAIGRETTE

8–10 stalks celery

½ cup rice vinegar

2 Tbsp. mirin

juice of ½ lemon

4 leaves shiso, finely julienned

⅓ cup finely diced celery

TAMARI-VINEGAR REDUCTION

¼ cup tamari

½ cup balsamic vinegar

TUNA CARPACCIO

8 oz. ahi tuna

lemon oil (see page 171)

extra virgin olive oil

pinch of fleur de sel or coarse sea salt

radishes, thinly sliced, for garnish

1 cup microgreens for garnish

lemon oil (see page 171) for garnish

ABOUT THE RECIPE: I love raw fish. The tuna in this recipe is accented by unusual flavors and textures. Shiso is the serrated leaf used to decorate plates in Japanese restaurants, but it's also used sometimes to give an interesting sharpness that complements ahi. If you can't use ahi tuna, substitute albacore.

TO PREPARE VINAIGRETTE: Make celery juice by passing cleaned celery stalks through an electric juicer or by puréeing celery in a food processor and draining the pulp through a cheesecloth-lined sieve to catch the juice. You will need ½ cup celery juice.

Combine the celery juice, rice vinegar, mirin and lemon juice and transfer to a shallow pan. Place in freezer and chill until partially frozen. Mash with a fork about every 20 minutes as it freezes. Continue doing this until you have a granité consistency.

TAMARI-VINEGAR REDUCTION: Combine tamari and balsamic vinegar in a small pot and simmer over medium heat, stirring occasionally, to reduce by half.

CARPACCIO: Cut the tuna into 4 rounds. Place each round between 2 sheets of plastic wrap and lightly pound to flatten as thin as possible, about ⅛-inch thick. Remove the top layer of plastic and invert tuna rounds onto serving plates, leaving the other plastic layer attached. Transfer the plates to the freezer and chill for at least 20 minutes.

TO ASSEMBLE: Remove the plastic wrap from the plated tuna and allow tuna to sit for 5 minutes. Drizzle with lemon oil and olive oil and spread to coat fish. Sprinkle with a pinch of coarse salt. Place a few slices of radish on top of the granité. In a small bowl, toss micro-greens with a little lemon oil. Mix shiso and celery into the granité, and place a spoonful on each tuna carpaccio. Place a bouquet of microgreens on top of dish. Drizzle a spoonful of tamari-vinegar reduction around the tuna.

WINE: An Italian Pinot Grigio or a Sancerre.

Serves 4

Citrus-cured sockeye salmon
and potato gnocchi with balsamic glaze

CITRUS-CURED SALMON

¼ cup + 2 Tbsp. kosher salt

4 Tbsp. white sugar

1 bunch dill, chopped

zest of 1 orange

juice and finely grated zest of 2 lemons

1 Tbsp. Dijon mustard

1 lb. or 1 side fresh salmon or
    Arctic char, filleted, pin bones
    removed, skin on

basic gnocchi (see page 173)

1 Tbsp. grapeseed oil

¾ cup chicken stock (see page 169)

1 tsp. white wine vinegar

2 Tbsp. unsalted butter

2 tsp. finely diced carrots

2 tsp. finely diced leeks or onion

2 tsp. finely diced celery

1 Tbsp. chopped chives

1 cup olive oil

balsamic glaze (see page 172) for garnish

mesclun greens (optional) for garnish

ABOUT THE RECIPE: Sweden is another place that taught me about simplicity. You can't get much simpler than Swedish food, and yet it's absolutely wonderful. I was introduced to gravlax, chanterelles and ice fishing there when I was an exchange student in the early 1980s.

Gravlax quickly became a favorite because of the texture and the balance of sweetness with a touch of acidity. My adaptation adds olive oil and serves it warm instead of cold.

TO PREPARE THE SALMON: To make the marinade, mix the salt, sugar, dill, zests, lemon juice and mustard. Lay the salmon flat in a shallow dish and spread the mixture over the surface of the fillet. Cover with plastic wrap. Leave to marinate in refrigerator for 24 hours. Wash off the marinade and pat the fish dry. Cover tightly and refrigerate until needed.

GNOCCHI: Make gnocchi according to directions on page 173. In a large nonstick frying pan, heat the grapeseed oil using just enough oil to coat the pan. Make sure the gnocchi are thoroughly dry, then add them to the pan. Toss the gnocchi for 1–2 minutes, or until slightly browned on both sides. Add the stock, vinegar and butter and simmer for a couple of minutes until the liquid reduces to a sauce consistency. Add the carrots, leeks or onions, celery and chives. Add salt and freshly ground white pepper to taste. Remove from heat.

TO ASSEMBLE: Just before serving, heat the salmon. You will need 1 cup olive oil in a small pot. Cut the salmon into 1-inch-wide strips. For each serving you will need 2 of these pieces of salmon.

To heat, bring the olive oil to a light simmer over medium heat. Take the oil off the heat and let it cool for 2–3 minutes. Immerse the salmon, which is already cooked from the marinade, in the oil and let sit for 2–3 minutes. Carefully remove warmed salmon from oil with a slotted spoon. Blot excess oil from surface with a paper towel.

To serve, divide the gnocchi mixture onto 4 plates and arrange 2 salmon strips on top. Drizzle the balsamic glaze around the outside and garnish with small greens.

WINE: A nice rich Pinot Gris; a British Columbia one would be lovely.

Serves 4 · photo, page 8

Seared Pacific cod with a fricassée of mussels, clams and chorizo with parsley oil

½ cup dry white wine

1 sprig thyme

1 small clove garlic, minced

½ small shallot, chopped

8 Pacific clams

8 Pacific mussels

1 link dry-cured chorizo sausage,
    cut into ½-inch slices

1 cup heavy cream

¼ cup diced celery, blanched

¼ cup diced Yukon Gold potatoes,
    blanched

lemon juice (optional)

one 2½-lb. fillet Pacific cod, skin on, scaled

4 Tbsp. vegetable oil

1 Tbsp. unsalted butter

4 Pacific oysters, freshly shucked

1 tsp. chopped flat-leaf parsley for garnish

2 Tbsp. parsley oil (see page 171)
    for garnish

ABOUT THE RECIPE: Cod is one of the most underrated fish available. In North America, most people think of it only as the cheap fish in fish and chips. But it's much more than that. Who says something has to cost a lot to be wonderful?

For this recipe we use Pacific cod, also known as grey cod, the only true cod species in the Pacific. The flesh is firm and sweet, but it has slightly more fat than Atlantic cod, so it works better in a braising or steaming situation than as a pan-fry.

TO PREPARE: Make the nectar in a large pot with a lid. Place the white wine, thyme, garlic, shallot, clams, mussels and chorizo in the pot, cover and bring to a boil. Do not mix or stir. Remove the shellfish as they open, about 2–3 minutes. Remove the meat from the shellfish. Reduce the liquid to a simmer. Strain so that you are left with about ½ cup of liquid. Taste the sauce to check for salt before seasoning. Add the cream, celery and potatoes. Season sauce to taste and add a touch of lemon juice if necessary.

Preheat oven to 450° F. Season cod with salt and freshly ground white pepper and cut into 4 portions. Heat vegetable oil in an ovenproof frying pan on medium-high heat until lightly smoking. Add cod, skin-side down. Sear on one side until lightly browned and turn over. Place in preheated oven for 2–3 minutes. Don't ever be afraid to poke the fish with your knife and look inside. The flesh should be translucent and moist.

TO ASSEMBLE: Shuck the oysters as close to serving time as possible. In a separate saucepan, heat the nectar over medium heat. Place the mussel and clam meat back in the sauce and just before serving add the oysters. They should be warmed rather than fully cooked. Oysters are salty so be careful when seasoning.

To serve, pour some sauce into 4 soup bowls, divide the mussel and clam meat and the oysters among the bowls then place a piece of cod in each bowl. Sprinkle with parsley and drizzle some parsley oil around the dish to garnish.

WINE: A rich, crisp white: Spanish Albariño or white Rioja.

Serves 4

Seared Pacific cod with a fricassée of mussels,
clams and chorizo with parsley oil (facing)

Seared halibut in a warm herb vinaigrette

½ tsp. Dijon mustard

1 small shallot, finely diced

1 cup house vinaigrette (see page 172)

1 Tbsp. grapeseed oil

four 4-oz. halibut pieces, skin on, scaled

½ tsp. chopped tarragon

1½ tsp. chopped flat-leaf parsley

2 Tbsp. chopped fresh chives

2 Tbsp. chopped fresh chervil

ABOUT THE RECIPE: Here's a very healthy way to eat this fish. Little fat, clean flavor—an idea inspired by Le Bernardin in New York City. It's so simple, yet you'll be surprised by the flavor of it. I like to serve this dish with steamed asparagus and Israeli couscous or simple gnocchi.

TO PREPARE: Put the mustard and shallot in a mixing bowl and slowly whisk in the vinaigrette. Transfer to a small saucepan and set aside. Preheat the oven to 350° F.

Heat the oil in a large ovenproof nonstick frying pan. Season both sides of the halibut with salt and freshly ground white pepper. Sear the halibut for 1–2 minutes on each side, starting with the skin side.

Place pan in the preheated oven and continue cooking the fish in the oven for a further 4–5 minutes. Remove the halibut from the oven when it has reached desired doneness.

Meanwhile, warm the vinaigrette sauce over low heat and chop and add the herbs at the last minute. Serve the halibut skin-side up. Sprinkle on a pinch of coarse salt and drizzle the vinaigrette around the dish.

WINE: A Sauvignon Blanc or a crisp cool-climate Chardonnay.

Serves 4

Broth and juice

Thick and goopy doesn't work for me. I love flavored broths, and
I have done so ever since I tasted miso soup at the next-door neigh-
bors' when I was a kid. The clarity of taste was a revelation. Later,
French onion soup, minus the bread and cheese, showed me how
intense a light soup can be.

How much purer can you get than a broth made by putting a
fruit or vegetable through a juicer? I'm a huge fan of juicers because
they give me that ability to push the elements, to change the form
but capture all the flavor. Now I can employ that flavor in unexpected
ways. These brilliant-flavored extracts—call them broths or juices
or waters—are at their best cold and fresh.

< *Chilled cucumber and watermelon
soup with Dungeness crab (page 51)*

Roasted poussin in a soy, icewine and mustard sauce with a potato pavé

POTATO PAVÉ

3 cups heavy cream

2 cloves garlic, peeled and crushed

pinch of nutmeg

3 Yukon Gold potatoes, peeled and very
     thinly sliced

1 Tbsp. vegetable oil

1 Tbsp. melted unsalted butter

POUSSIN

2 poussins or Cornish game hens

8 sprigs thyme

4 small cloves garlic

4 Tbsp. softened unsalted butter

SAUCE

2 cups icewine or white dessert wine

1 Tbsp. rice vinegar

2 Tbsp. soy sauce

1 Tbsp. grainy mustard

2 Tbsp. unsalted butter

1 or 2 tsp. lemon juice

4 tsp. parsley oil (see page 171)
     for garnish

ABOUT THE RECIPE: Roast chicken and potatoes—what could be more Canadian? If anything, adding a couple of subtle Japanese influences makes it even more Canadian.

A poussin is a young, small chicken—about 9–11 ounces. Roasting the baby chicken on the bone keeps it tender and prevents it from drying out because all the moisture is close to the bones.

TO PREPARE POTATO PAVÉ: Prepare pavé at least 6 hours ahead of time. Preheat the oven to 350° F. In a large pot over medium heat, simmer cream, garlic, nutmeg, a couple of pinches of salt and freshly ground white pepper. Reduce by one-third.

Blanch potato slices in seasoned cream until three-quarters cooked. Cook about half a potato's worth of slices at a time. Remove slices with slotted spoon.

Brush a loaf pan with vegetable oil. Overlap potato slices slightly in a layer in the pan. Season with salt and freshly ground white pepper. Continue layering until all the potatoes are used. Tightly cover the potatoes with a sheet of aluminum foil. Place another loaf pan over the foil and push down to compact the potatoes. Remove foil and reserve for later. Drizzle butter over potatoes. Bake for 35–45 minutes, or until the potatoes are golden brown on top and tender when tested with a knife.

Allow pavé to cool for 30 minutes. Place foil on top and compact pavé again by pressing on top with a loaf pan. Refrigerate for at least 4 hours.

POUSSIN: Preheat the oven to 375° F. To roast the poussins, season the cavities with salt and freshly ground white pepper, and place 4 thyme sprigs and 2 crushed garlic cloves in the cavity of each bird. Rub the skin with the softened butter and season with salt and freshly ground white pepper. Place birds in the refrigerator to harden the butter.

Place the poussins on a rack in a large roasting pan and roast them for 45 minutes, or until the juices run clear. Remove from the oven and allow to rest for 10 minutes before carving the leg and the breast meat.

SAUCE: In a wide pan, combine wine, vinegar and soy sauce and reduce by one-third over medium heat. Strain mixture through a fine-mesh sieve into a small pot. Add mustard and bring to a simmer.

Reduce heat and slowly whisk in the butter, a bit at a time. Season sauce with lemon juice, salt and freshly ground white pepper. Keep warm.

TO ASSEMBLE: Before serving, cut pavé into desired shapes. Place 4 portions on a plate, each with a dab of butter on top. Place in the microwave at medium to medium-high heat for 1–2 minutes, or place on a pan in a 375° F oven for 5 minutes or until warmed through. Remove the breasts and leg-and-thigh sections of the poussins.

To serve, place a square of pavé in the center of each plate, arrange one breast and one leg-and-thigh section on top. Spoon some of the sauce over and around, add a drizzle parsley oil. Serve immediately.

WINE: A rich Gewürztraminer, or a lighter Pinot Noir or Côtes du Rhône.

Serves 4

*Herb-crusted beef tenderloin with chanterelles
and a shallot and caper jus (facing)*

Herb-crusted beef tenderloin with chanterelles and a shallot and caper jus

JUS
1 Tbsp. unsalted butter
4 shallots, finely chopped
¼ cup red wine
2 cups veal reduction (see page 167)
1 Tbsp. capers, rinsed

HERB CRUST
2 Tbsp. flat-leaf parsley, coarsely chopped
2 Tbsp. unsalted butter, melted
1 Tbsp. olive oil
¾ cup Japanese Panko crumbs

3 Tbsp. chopped parsley
2 Tbsp. fresh thyme leaves
1 Tbsp. fresh tarragon, coarsely chopped

TENDERLOIN
four 4-oz. portions beef tenderloin
2 Tbsp. vegetable oil

CHANTERELLES
2 Tbsp. unsalted butter
½ lb. chanterelle mushrooms, trimmed
and cleaned
1 clove garlic, minced

ABOUT THE RECIPE: It's common enough to put a crust on a rack of lamb but, for some reason, people seldom think of it for beef. I find the crust gives beef another dimension, and the shallot and caper jus gives it a little hit of acid. I like to serve it with any roasted potato.

TO PREPARE JUS: In a saucepan over medium heat, melt the butter and sauté the shallots. Remove 1 Tbsp. shallots and set aside. Deglaze pan with wine and reduce by two-thirds or until slightly syrupy. Add the veal reduction and reduce by another one-third. Strain through a fine-mesh sieve. Add capers and reserved shallots. Set aside.

    HERB CRUST: Preheat oven to 400° F. Mix together all herb crust ingredients and season with salt and freshly ground black pepper.

    TENDERLOIN: Season the beef tenderloins with salt and freshly ground black pepper. Heat an ovenproof frying pan over high heat and add vegetable oil. When hot, add the tenderloins and sear on each side for 2 minutes or until brown. Remove from heat and firmly pack herb crust on one side. Transfer to oven and roast to medium rare (115–120° F internal temperature) or until desired doneness. Remove from oven, cover loosely with aluminum foil and allow to rest at least 10 minutes.

    CHANTERELLES: Heat a sauté pan over high heat, melt butter and add chanterelles and garlic. Cook until golden brown.

TO ASSEMBLE: Place a portion of potato pavé (see page 66) or other roasted potato in center of 4 large plates. Spoon some chanterelles around. Cut the tenderloin in half horizontally and arrange on top of the potato. Spoon warm shallot and caper jus over chanterelles. Sprinkle a pinch of fleur de sel on the beef.

WINE: A rich Italian red.

Serves 4

Foie gras torchon with vanilla brioche and wine-poached peaches

FOIE GRAS

1–1¼ lbs. Grade-A fresh foie gras

milk

1 tsp. fleur de sel or coarse sea salt

⅛ tsp. freshly ground white pepper

½ Tbsp. sugar

pinch of saltpeter (optional)

2 qts. chicken stock (see page 169)

BRIOCHE

1 Tbsp. active dry yeast

¼ cup sugar

4 Tbsp. warm water (140° F)

6 large eggs

4 cups sifted all-purpose flour

pulp of 1 vanilla bean

1 Tbsp. salt

2 cups unsalted butter,
    softened

POACHED PEACHES

1 cup icewine or other dessert wine

2 peaches

¼ cup water

ABOUT THE RECIPE: My search for the perfect foie gras recipe is a lifetime project. The idea for this dish came from the experiences I had working in Alsace at Au Crocodile. There, Emile Jung offered a *foie gras torchon* (which means wrapped in cloth), and I found it the purest way to experience the full flavor of a foie gras.

Making this dish is a 3-day process. The seasoning is very important: it should be subtle enough to bring out the natural sweetness of the meat. Once the foie gras is cooked, the flavor gets better if it is stored in the refrigerator for up to a week.

Torchon requires the best quality foie gras because it is so lightly seasoned. Lesser grades benefit from the addition of other flavors like cognac or other liquors, but a fine top-quality foie gras doesn't need much help.

Saltpeter, also known as pink salt, is potassium nitrate. It's used in preserving meat and will give the foie gras a nice pink color. Saltpeter is available at drugstores.

TO PREPARE FOIE GRAS: Rinse the foie gras under cold water, pat it dry and place it in a container. Add enough milk to cover the foie gras completely, cover and refrigerate for about 24 hours. This step allows the blood to pass into the milk.

To clean the foie gras, remove it from the milk and rinse it under cold water. Pat dry and place on a plate until it becomes pliable, about 10 minutes. Pull the two lobes apart. Heat a sharp knife and slice each lobe in half horizontally. This will expose the veins. Using tweezers, grasp the ends of the veins, pulling to remove them. It doesn't matter if you break up the foie gras as you search for veins. Continue with the other lobe. When you have removed as many veins as possible, reassemble the foie gras.

Place the foie gras on a parchment-lined baking sheet. Mix the coarse salt, white pepper, sugar and saltpeter, and sprinkle over the foie gras. Place plastic wrap over foie gras and press down to remove any air pockets (any air will discolor the surface). Wrap tightly with plastic wrap, pressing the mixture into the foie gras. Refrigerate overnight.

To shape the foie gras for cooking, remove from fridge and let it sit until it is a bit pliable and won't break when you move it. Place foie gras on a sheet of parchment and roll into a log, squeezing it together so you can get rid of any air pockets inside. Twist both ends of the paper to remove any air pockets and make a firm cylinder. Remove the paper and place the foie gras on some cheesecloth. Roll it away from you until it is wrapped in the cloth. Tie the ends of the cheesecloth with kitchen twine, then secure the cylinder with string every 3 inches. The torchon should be 12–18 inches long. Refrigerate until ready to cook.

To cook, bring the stock to a boil in a stockpot or fish poacher large enough to hold the whole torchon. Immerse the foie gras in the boiling stock, reduce stock to a simmer and cook for 1½ minutes. Pull torchon out immediately and plunge into an ice bath. Once it is cool, roll the torchon in a sheet of aluminum foil. Twist both ends until the roll is so firm you cannot twist anymore. This will reshape the cylinder. Remove the foil and place roll in a baking tray. Slide a plate under one end of the torchon to tilt it and allow any excess stock to escape. Refrigerate overnight.

BRIOCHE: Dissolve the yeast and 2 Tbsp. of the sugar in the warm water. Mix well. Leave in a warm place until it is foamy and all the yeast has dissolved, from 5–8 minutes.

Use a heavy-duty mixer with a paddle attachment. Break the eggs into the mixing bowl. Cover with 2 cups flour.

Mix the vanilla pulp and remaining sugar. Add them in another layer, and add salt to one side of the bowl. Cover this layer with the remaining flour. Dig a shallow well in the flour—don't dig into the sugar/salt layer because the salt will kill the yeast. Put bloomed yeast in well and place bowl on mixer platform. Mix, slowly at first to combine ingredients, then beat at medium-high speed until mixture comes away from sides of bowl, about 5 minutes.

Pull dough off paddle and reduce speed to medium. Add butter 1 Tbsp. at a time while dough is mixing. Keep mixing for 5–10 minutes until the dough pulls away from the sides of the bowl and looks very smooth. Remove from mixer, cover and refrigerate overnight.

On a floured surface, shape dough for brioche molds or loaf pan. Cover and put in a warm place until dough has doubled in size.

Preheat the oven to 350° F. Place molds or pans on a baking sheet and bake for 15 minutes, then give the sheet a half-turn to assure even baking. Bake 10–20 minutes longer until the outside is crisp and the loaf sounds hollow when tapped. The brioche can be wrapped tightly in plastic wrap and frozen for a month.

POACHED PEACHES: In a small pot, bring wine and water to a boil. Peel peaches and slice into wedges. Place peaches in syrup and allow to macerate for 10 minutes. Remove peaches and reserve syrup in the refrigerator for another purpose.

TO ASSEMBLE: Just before serving, cut the brioche into 16 slices. Toast the brioche slices until golden brown. Cut the torchon into ½-inch slices with a hot knife. Reheat knife and gently slide hot knife over the surface of the foie gras to glaze. Overlap 3 foie gras slices on each plate and sprinkle each slice with a few grains of fleur de sel. Arrange toasted brioche slices around foie gras and spoon peaches on the side. Serve immediately.

WINE: A late-harvest Riesling or Gewürztraminer or a Sauternes.

Serves 8

Coulommiers cheese with a watercress and watermelon salad

four 1-oz. portions Coulommiers cheese
handful baby watercress, washed and dried
¼ cup diced watermelon
3 Tbsp. toasted pumpkin seeds
lemon oil (see page 171) for garnish

ABOUT THE RECIPE: Coulommiers is a small brie which makes it the perfect size for a small group of people.

TO ASSEMBLE: Place cheese on individual plates. Arrange a small mound of watercress beside the cheese and sprinkle with diced watermelon and pumpkin seeds. Drizzle with lemon oil.

WINE: A rich French red: Bordeaux, Rhône or Burgundy.

Serves 4

Brie de Meaux cheese with candied tomatoes

1 cup cherry tomatoes, halved
¼ cup sugar
juice of ½ lemon
4 oz. Brie de Meaux cheese

ABOUT THE RECIPE: A mature Brie de Meaux is perhaps the most flavorful of all the brie cheeses. The candied tomatoes cut the creaminess.

TO PREPARE: Place tomato halves in a bowl and sprinkle with sugar. Cover and place in refrigerator overnight. Drain off excess liquid and transfer to a small saucepan. Gently cook uncovered over low heat for 2–3 minutes, or until softened but still intact. Add lemon juice, remove from heat and set aside to cool. Cover and refrigerate until ready to use.

To assemble, divide the brie into 4 small wedges and place on individual serving plates. Add a small spoonful of the candied tomatoes on the side of the cheese and serve.

WINE: A rich, complex red: Bordeaux or Côte de Nuits or a northern Rhône Syrah.

Serves 4

Warm chocolate cake with
sweet corn ice cream (page 123)

Reblochon cheese with kumquat marmalade

½ lb. kumquats (2½ cups)
¼ cup orange segments, skin and membranes removed
½ vanilla bean, split and pulped

1 cup granulated sugar
juice of 1 lemon
four 1-oz. portions Reblochon cheese
4 slices fruit-and-nut bread

ABOUT THE RECIPE: You can tell Reblochon comes from a mountain area—it has that same nuttiness you find in a Swiss cheese, but with the French creaminess. This comes from the Savoie region of France and is one of my favorite cheeses.

TO PREPARE: Slice kumquats into ¼ to ½-inch-thick coins. Remove seeds from both kumquats and orange segments. Combine in a large pot with vanilla bean and pulp, sugar and lemon juice. Place over medium heat. Bring mixture to a boil; reduce heat and simmer, stirring occasionally, for 20 minutes until slightly thickened. Remove vanilla bean, transfer marmalade to a glass container and allow to cool. Refrigerate until ready to use.

Place Reblochon on individual plates. Serve with a small portion of the kumquat marmalade and a slice of fruit-and-nut bread.

WINE: A sticky Sauternes or Barsac from France, late-harvest Semillon from Australia.

Serves 4 · photo, page 156

Lemon and basil tart with lemon sorbet

CITRUS SHORTBREAD CRUST

½ lb. unsalted butter,
    room temperature
½ cup castor or berry sugar
1½ cups all-purpose flour
pinch of salt
zest of ½ lemon
zest of ½ lime
zest of ½ orange

LEMON BASIL FILLING

¼ lb. unsalted butter (½ cup)
¼ cup heavy cream
2 eggs
2 egg yolks
¾ cup fresh lemon juice, strained
¾ cup granulated sugar
½ cup packed fresh basil leaves

confectioners' sugar for garnish
lemon sorbet (see page 176) for garnish

ABOUT THE RECIPE: The *tarte au citron*, when it's done correctly, is one of the world's great desserts. François Payard of Payard Pâtisserie and Bistro in New York makes one of the best, and I learned his techniques when I attended one of his cooking classes. He later visited Lumière and really enjoyed a lemon and basil sorbet we served. Out of that came his suggestion to add basil to a tarte au citron to make a completely different—and inspired— dessert. I adapted this from his idea.

TO PREPARE CRUST: Preheat oven to 300°–325° F. Cream the butter using a heavy-duty electric mixer with paddle attachment. Gradually add sugar until combined. Slowly add flour, salt and zests, and mix at medium-high until combined. Scrape dough from the sides of the bowl to form a ball.

Roll dough out to ⅛-inch thickness. Line four 3-inch tart tins with dough, or line an 8-inch springform pan. Dough should come up the sides at least 1 inch. Pierce dough all over with a fork. Blind bake 8–10 minutes (longer for a larger pan). There should be little or no color. Cool on a rack. Remove tart shells from tins.

FILLING: Heat butter and cream in a double boiler over boiling water. In a separate bowl, beat eggs and egg yolks together just enough to blend. Temper the eggs with a small amount of the warm cream mixture and add eggs to remaining cream mixture. Heat over boiling water, whisking constantly, until lukewarm. Whisk in lemon juice and granulated sugar. Stir in basil. Continue cooking, whisking every few minutes so mixture does not curdle. Cook until mixture reaches a custardlike consistency (180° F), about 15–20 minutes. Remove from heat and strain through a fine-mesh sieve into a clean bowl and let it cool for 10 minutes.

Preheat oven to 250° F. Place tart shells on a baking sheet and fill with custard. Bake until custard sets, about 10 minutes. Remove from oven and allow to cool before handling.

To serve, place tarts or tart slices on individual plates, dust with confectioners' sugar and garnish with a scoop of lemon sorbet.

WINE: Madeira, the older the better.

Serves 4

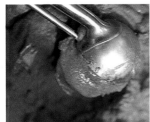

Blueberry sorbet (page 175) with
lemon and tarragon jus (page 179)

Orange bavarois with mango sauce

ORANGE JELLY

1 Tbsp. gelatin

¾ cup + 1 Tbsp. strained fresh orange juice

¾ cup simple syrup (see page 175)

CUSTARD

4 tsp. gelatin

¾ cup + 1 Tbsp. strained fresh orange juice

1 cup 2% milk

1½ cups sugar

8 large egg yolks

2 cups heavy cream

MANGO SAUCE

2 large ripe mangoes, peeled and cut
 into chunks

2 Tbsp. simple syrup (see page 175)

¼ cup strained fresh orange juice

ABOUT THE RECIPE: Orange bavarois is creamy but with a beautiful light, clean finish—the perfect little sugar rush to end a summer meal before you head off on a walk along the beach or out for a last game of Frisbee. Try it also with blood oranges or honey tangerines.

TO PREPARE ORANGE JELLY: In a medium heatproof bowl, combine gelatin and 3 Tbsp. of the orange juice. Set aside.

In a small pot combine remaining orange juice and simple syrup. Bring to a boil over high heat. Remove from heat and pour a small amount over the gelatin mixture. Whisk until gelatin dissolves. Add remaining orange juice mixture and whisk to combine. Place twelve ¾-cup custard cups or ramekins on a baking sheet. Spoon about 2 Tbsp. of the gelatin mixture into each. Refrigerate uncovered for at least 1 hour or until set.

CUSTARD: In a small heatproof bowl, combine gelatin and 3 Tbsp. of the orange juice. Set aside. In medium saucepan, combine milk, 1 cup of the sugar and remaining orange juice. Bring mixture to a boil over medium-high heat, whisking occasionally (the curdled appearance will disappear after boiling). Remove from heat. Whisk one quarter of the hot milk mixture into gelatin mixture.

In a medium heatproof bowl, whisk yolks with remaining ½ cup sugar. Gradually whisk a small amount of the hot milk mixture into the yolks. Pour gelatin and yolk mixtures into the hot milk mixture. Cook, stirring constantly, over medium heat for about 10 minutes, or until custard coats the back of a spoon. Do not allow the mixture to boil. Strain custard into a large heatproof bowl. Place bowl in an ice bath and let custard cool, stirring frequently.

In large bowl, whip cream until firm peaks form. Gently fold cooled custard into whipped cream. Spoon ½ cup of the mixture into each ramekin on top of the set orange jelly. Refrigerate for at least 2 hours or until set. These can be covered and refrigerated overnight.

MANGO SAUCE: Purée mango, simple syrup and orange juice together until smooth, adding more juice to thin the sauce if necessary. Strain through a fine-mesh sieve into a bowl and set aside. This can be covered and refrigerated for up to 3 days.

TO ASSEMBLE: Working quickly, dip each ramekin partway into a bowl of very hot water. Run a sharp, flexible knife around the inside edge. Invert onto a dessert plate. Drizzle about 1 Tbsp. of mango sauce around each bavarois. Pass any remaining sauce separately.

WINE: Something marmalade-y: a Corsican Muscat; or an Alsace late-harvest Pinot Gris.

Serves 12

Goat cheesecake in a praline crust
with cherry port sauce

PRALINE CRUST

2 oz. white chocolate, roughly chopped

6 oz. praline paste (available at
    specialty bakery supply stores)

2 oz. feuillantine (available at specialty
    bakery supply stores) or cornflakes

GOAT CHEESE FILLING

14 oz. fresh goat cheese, softened at
    room temperature

one 8-oz. pkg. cream cheese, softened,
    at room temperature (do not use
    whipped variety)

¾ cup sugar

⅔ cup heavy cream

6 large eggs

SAUCE

1 cup dried cherries

¾ cup cherry juice

¼ cup ruby port

1 tsp. cornstarch dissolved in
    1 Tbsp. cold water

ABOUT THE RECIPE: Every year Andrew Quady, the maker of some of California's best dessert wines and ports, holds a dessert contest in Vancouver that challenges chefs to match a particular wine. Three years ago the wine was a port that was very rich in berry tones. Because goat cheese and port go so well together, we took it another step and made goat cheese the foundation of this unusual cheesecake. We won first place.

We make it in single portions, but I've also given directions for one large cheesecake.

TO PREPARE CRUST: In a double boiler over simmering water, melt chocolate and praline paste together. Stir in the cereal and mix well to combine. Spread the chocolate-praline mixture onto a parchment-lined baking sheet. Place another sheet of parchment on top of the mixture and roll with a rolling pin until ⅛-inch thick. (For a large cheesecake, roll the crust in a rough circle at least 8 inches across.) Transfer the crust to freezer and chill for ½ hour.

Remove crust from freezer and carefully remove the top parchment from the chocolate. Using a round metal cutter, cut the crust to fit 8–12 individual ramekins. Heat the cutter and make sure it is dry. (For a large cheesecake, use the ring of an 8-inch springform pan as your guide and cut with a hot, dry knife.) Set crusts aside.

FILLING: Preheat oven to 250° F. With an electric mixer beat the goat cheese, cream cheese and sugar until smooth. Stir in cream just to incorporate. Scrape down the bowl as you stir to incorporate all the cheese and prevent lumps.

In a separate bowl, lightly beat the eggs. Gradually mix half the beaten eggs into the cheese mixture until combined. Scrape down the bowl and add remaining eggs.

Butter and sugar the sides of the ramekins or springform pan. Seal the outside of the springform pan with foil to prevent any water from getting in. Pour in filling. Place ramekins or pan in a shallow pan with water halfway up the sides. Bake in water bath for 25 minutes, 45 minutes for large cheesecake.

Remove and let cool at room temperature. To prevent the large cheesecake from cracking, invert a bowl over the pan as the cake cools. When cool, cover with plastic wrap and refrigerate.

SAUCE: In a small pot, combine cherries, cherry juice and port. Bring to a boil. Remove from heat and allow to cool.

Whisk half the cornstarch mixture into cherry liquid. Return to boil, reduce heat and simmer until sauce thickens, about 2 minutes. If it hasn't thickened to the point that it will coat the back of a spoon, remove from heat. Stir 1 Tbsp. of the cherry liquid into the remaining cornstarch mixture, then return to cherry liquid. Return liquid to boil and simmer 2 minutes or until sauce is thickened and clear.

TO ASSEMBLE: Place praline crusts on plates. Unmold cheesecake onto crusts. For large cheesecake, cut wedges of crust with a hot, dry knife. Place wedges of cheesecake on top. Arrange a few cherries on top of cheesecake and spoon sauce and more cherries around.

WINE: A Pedro Ximénez sherry, Australian dessert Muscat or Vin Santo.

Serves 8 to 12

{ A U T U M N }

EVERYTHING CHANGES once I see the pumpkins. They seem to just appear one day, an orange surprise in fields that used to be indistinguishable from the ones around them. That's when it's time for a whole new scenario in cooking.

In spring and summer, getting the true flavor out of ingredients means the less cooking the better. With the autumn crop of root vegetables and squashes I have to extract flavor in a different way. I go for the fuller tones that come from slow cooking—the sugars that emerge in roasting, the depth that braising develops.

In the autumn, aromas of roasted meat remind me of Sunday dinners surrounded by family. Soups want a bit of substance; a clear broth won't do the trick anymore. The wealth of mushrooms, particularly chanterelles, inspires me. And with the short days and chilly evenings, everything demands to be served warm—even the salads.

VEGETABLE MENU

Baby greens salad with goat cheese,
walnuts, shaved Parmesan and a honey-
blossom vinaigrette   *90*

Pumpkin soup with pumpkin seeds,
rye croutons and a lightly whipped
nutmeg cream   *85*

Herb ravioli with chanterelles,
tomato coulis and basil oil   *92*

Chanterelles with napa cabbage rolls
and rosemary crème fraîche in a
mushroom emulsion   *94*

Selles-sur-Cher cheese with
quince jelly   *117*

Lime sorbet with banana
and vanilla jus   *176, 178*

Spice cake with espresso dark rum
ice cream   *119*

SIGNATURE MENU

Clam and mussel chowder with
a curry froth   *86*

Heirloom tomato salad with goat cheese
cream and a light balsamic vinaigrette   *91*

Seared spot prawns with puréed potatoes
and a lemon and tobiko beurre blanc   *101*

Braised sweetbreads with truffled
green lentils   *114*

Roasted duck with duck confit,
Israeli couscous and a warm soy-ginger
vinaigrette   *106*

Squab wrapped in potato with seared
foie gras, squab jus and a garlic froth   *110*

Seared lamb loin with baekenofe   *112*

Beaufort cheese with poached figs   *118*

Lychee and champagne sorbet   *176*

Warm chocolate cake with sweet
corn ice cream   *123*

SEAFOOD MENU

Oysters on the half shell with tomato,
daikon and cucumber relish   *97*

Seared scallops with baby leeks
and blue cluster chanterelles in
herb vinaigrette   *98*

Butter-braised Atlantic lobster with lobster
bisque and mascarpone risotto   *102*

Seared Arctic char with cauliflower purée
and a smoked sablefish and horseradish
emulsion   *105*

Epoisses de Bourgogne cheese
with macerated fruit   *117*

Citrus sorbet with
cardamom jus   *176, 179*

Fig tatin with Sambuca ice cream   *122*

*Five-spice duck consommé with duck confit
and caramelized onion ravioli (page 130)*

Pumpkin soup with pumpkin seeds, rye croutons and a lightly whipped nutmeg cream

2 Tbsp. unsalted butter

½ small white onion, thinly sliced

1 stalk celery, thinly sliced

2 cloves garlic, thinly sliced

2 sprigs thyme

1 bay leaf

1 small sweet pumpkin, peel and seeds
    removed, cut into small chunks
    (about 4 cups)

⅓ cup dry white wine

4 cups vegetable stock (see page 170)

3 Tbsp. unsalted butter

¼ cup heavy cream

¼ tsp. ground nutmeg

⅓ cup rye bread croutons

1 Tbsp. toasted, salted pumpkin seeds

ABOUT THE RECIPE: All of our soups are basically purées that deliver the essence of the main ingredient. Here is fall in a bowl: just the natural sugar of the pumpkin with the other ingredients adding some depth.

TO PREPARE: Over medium heat, melt the 2 Tbsp. butter in a large pot. Add the onion, celery, garlic, thyme and bay leaf and cook for 2–3 minutes until soft. Add pumpkin and allow it to sweat until it just begins to soften. Deglaze with wine. Add the stock, bring to a boil and simmer for 20 minutes or until pumpkin is very tender.

Cool soup and then purée in a blender. Pass purée through a fine-mesh sieve. Return to pot and heat over medium heat, seasoning with salt and freshly ground white pepper. If soup is too thick, thin it with more stock. Reduce heat to low and keep warm. Before serving, whisk in butter, a little at a time, to finish.

In a small bowl, whip the cream to soft-peak stage. Add nutmeg and season with a pinch of salt.

To serve, spoon soup into 4 soup plates, and sprinkle with croutons and pumpkin seeds. Serve the cream in a small bowl at the table.

WINE: A Pinot Gris—ideally a rich and spicy Alsace.

Serves 4

Clam and mussel chowder
with a curry froth

CURRY FROTH

1 Tbsp. unsalted butter

⅓ cup sliced onions

1 pear or apple, peeled, cored and
    thinly sliced

2 cloves garlic, finely chopped

1 bay leaf

2 sprigs thyme

1 Tbsp. curry powder

1 tsp. ground turmeric

¼ cup chicken stock (see page 169)

½ cup heavy cream

½ tsp. lemon juice

CHOWDER

¼ cup diced celery

⅓ cup diced Yukon Gold potatoes

⅓ cup diced carrot

1 lb. small fresh clams (such as Manila)

1 lb. fresh mussels

1 clove garlic

½ shallot

1 sprig thyme

¼ cup dry white wine

¼ cup chicken stock (see page 169)

1 cup heavy cream

1 Tbsp. unsalted butter

lemon juice, to taste

parsley oil (see page 171) for garnish

ABOUT THE RECIPE: Driving down to San Francisco or Monterey, or even as far as San Diego, you'll find chowders all the way. They're a West Coast staple. I love the flavor of mussel and clam soups, and the curry froth just adds new dimensions in taste and texture. We have a wonderful array of both clams and mussels here in British Columbia, and I can't think of a better way to combine them.

TO PREPARE CURRY FROTH: In a saucepan, melt the butter over medium heat. Add the onions, pear or apple, garlic, bay leaf and thyme. Sweat mixture until the vegetables are soft. Stir in the curry powder, turmeric and stock. Simmer to reduce by one-third. Add cream and bring to boil. Remove bay leaf and thyme. Purée in a blender and strain the mixture. Mixture should be just thick enough to coat the back of a spoon. If too thin, add more stock. Season with salt and freshly ground white pepper and add lemon juice.

CHOWDER: Blanch the celery, potatoes and carrots separately in boiling, salted water until just tender. Immediately plunge them into ice-cold water to stop the cooking. Drain well, then mix. Set aside.

Place the clams and mussels in a large pot with the garlic, shallot, thyme, wine and stock. Cover and bring to a light boil over medium heat until the clams and mussels have opened. Remove from heat. Strain the liquid into a pot. Remove the clam and mussel meat from shells and set aside.

Reduce the reserved liquid by about half. Add cream and bring to a boil. Remove from heat and whisk in butter. Season with salt and freshly ground white pepper and add lemon juice.

TO ASSEMBLE: Add the reserved clam and mussel meat to the liquid and heat to a simmer. Bring the curry cream almost to a simmer. Using a hand blender, foam curry cream until it is frothy. To serve, divide vegetable mix among 4 bowls. Put a spoonful of the curry froth on top of the vegetables. Ladle the hot soup into the bowls. Place a dollop of remaining curry froth on the soup. Garnish with a drizzle of parsley oil around the soup. Serve immediately.

WINE: A white Rhône or a richer-style Pinot Blanc.

Serves 4

Mise en place

Hours before the guests show up, hours before some of the cooks show up, a restaurant kitchen is a busy place. Vegetables are being diced, stocks are simmering, meat is being cut and fish are being filleted. When the service starts, everything that every station needs will be where it belongs, ready to go. That's *mise en place*, literally, "put in place," or a fancy way of saying you'd better be organized. It was the first term I learned in cooking school, and probably the most important lesson.

At home, mise en place will make you a more relaxed cook. It all begins with reading the recipe as a whole and breaking it down into its elements: "Okay, I'm going to braise some Belgian endive here and reduce some blood orange juice and cut up some blood oranges and a bit of cheese and sprinkle a few walnuts around."

All the recipes here are written in detail, but if you know what you're aiming at, you don't have to refer to the page at every step. Think of all the elements that will make up your meal and plan your order. You'll know what you can prepare ahead so that you're not desperately trying to caramelize onions in 3 minutes because you needed them 10 minutes ago.

Get everything ready to go. When you've done your prep and you know what you still need to do and in what order, you'll look just like one of those television chefs as you create fabulous things in your kitchen.

< *Warm endive and blood-orange salad with*
Roquefort cheese and walnuts (page 133)

Baby greens salad with goat cheese, walnuts, shaved Parmesan and a honey-blossom vinaigrette

VINAIGRETTE

4 Tbsp. fresh orange juice

1½ tsp. honey-blossom vinegar or
    1½ tsp. fine white wine or sherry
    vinegar mixed with 1 tsp.
    wildflower honey

¼ cup extra virgin olive oil

SALAD

1 head baby lollo rosso lettuce

1 head baby red oak leaf lettuce

1 head baby butter lettuce

⅓ cup walnut halves, toasted

⅓ cup freshly shaved Parmesan cheese curls

4 oz. soft goat cheese (½ cup)

ABOUT THE RECIPE: In this perfect salad, the fresh flavor of young, tender greens contrasts with the nutty saltiness of the Parmesan and the slight acidity of the goat cheese.

At Lumière, I have the luxury of using fine Doktorenhof vinegars which I import specially. This vinegar is made with very good quality wines from Germany and subtle infusions, such as vanilla, honey and even coffee, which are wonderful with the greens. You can make your own infusions by adding a split vanilla pod or some whole coffee beans to a good quality white wine or sherry vinegar, and letting them infuse in a dark cool area.

TO PREPARE VINAIGRETTE: Combine orange juice with vinegar and slowly whisk in oil. Season with salt and pepper; set aside.

SALAD: Thoroughly rinse and clean lettuces in cold water, dry well and set aside. If the leaves are large, tear them into smaller pieces but I usually prefer to use them whole. In a large bowl, combine lettuces with walnuts. Spoon in some of the vinaigrette. Season with salt and freshly ground white pepper.

TO ASSEMBLE: Divide and place some of the salad in the center of 4 large dinner plates. Arrange Parmesan shavings on the top. Crumble the goat cheese around the salad.

WINE: Any rich, sassy white that makes you smile.

Serves 4 · photo, page 132

Heirloom tomato salad with goat cheese cream and a light balsamic vinaigrette

GOAT CHEESE CREAM
6 Tbsp. soft fresh mild goat cheese
⅓ cup heavy cream

VINAIGRETTE
1 shallot, finely diced
2 Tbsp. aged balsamic vinegar
½ cup extra virgin olive oil

3–4 medium heirloom tomatoes
coarse sea salt
cracked black pepper
2 Tbsp. finely julienned basil
½ cup mixed baby greens for garnish
½ cup mixed fresh herbs, such as chives,
      parsley, basil, for garnish

ABOUT THE RECIPE: When I was a child, my family often vacationed in one of British Columbia's most popular holiday spots, the Okanagan—a desert only four hours from the lush green of Vancouver. The Okanagan Valley is renowned for its long growing season, which yields apples, stone fruits (cherries, peaches, apricots, plums) and grapes. The vast crop of grapes has made the Okanagan one of Canada's premier wine-growing areas.

This area has also been a source of tomatoes for many years, and recent interest in heirloom tomatoes has sparked farmers such as Stoney Paradise Farm's Milan Djordjevich to grow long-forgotten varieties, such as the green striped Zebra and the dark burgundy Black tomatoes. These tomatoes can be found at the various farmers' markets throughout the province during the growing season.

TO PREPARE GOAT CHEESE CREAM: Whisk together 2 Tbsp. goat cheese and the cream. The mixture should be thin enough to pour but thick enough not to run. Season with salt and freshly ground white pepper; set aside. Reserve remaining cheese to crumble over salad.

VINAIGRETTE: Combine shallots and vinegar, and slowly add oil, whisking constantly. This dressing does not have to be fully bound or emulsified. Season with salt and freshly ground white pepper.

TO ASSEMBLE: Cut tomatoes into small wedges and place in a bowl. Gently toss with the vinaigrette. Season with coarse sea salt and freshly cracked black pepper. Pile tomatoes on individual plates and sprinkle on a pinch more coarse salt. Crumble remaining goat cheese on tomatoes. Drizzle some of the goat cheese cream around the outside of the salad. Top with a small salad of mixed greens and herbs.

WINE: A Sauvignon Blanc, the crisper the better.

Serves 4 to 6

Herb ravioli with chanterelles, tomato coulis and basil oil

RAVIOLI

1½ tsp. olive oil

½ cup finely diced onions

1 clove garlic, finely chopped

½ lb. spinach, leaves only (2 cups)

3 Tbsp. chopped chives

3 Tbsp. chopped chervil

3 sprigs tarragon, leaves only,
  finely chopped

3 Tbsp. mascarpone cheese

2 Tbsp. ricotta cheese

3 Tbsp. finely grated Parmesan cheese

pinch of ground nutmeg

¼ recipe pasta dough (see page 173)

TOMATO COULIS

1 Tbsp. olive oil

½ cup onions, finely chopped

3 cloves garlic, finely chopped

1 bay leaf

1 sprig fresh thyme

one 14-oz. can plum tomatoes,
  drained and squeezed,
  excess juice reserved

3 lbs. ripe tomatoes, halved, seeded
  and finely chopped

pinch of sugar

4 sprigs basil

1 Tbsp. finely grated Parmesan cheese

1 Tbsp. unsalted butter

1 cup fresh chanterelles

1 Tbsp. basil oil (see page 171)
  for garnish

ABOUT THE RECIPE: All natural and packed with flavor, these ravioli were inspired by a dish I had at Daniel Boulud's restaurant in New York.

These ravioli are time consuming to make. They are best fresh, if you have the time, but they can be made in advance and frozen in resealable bags.

TO PREPARE RAVIOLI: In a small saucepan, heat the oil over medium heat and sweat the onions and garlic uncovered. Do not allow to color. Cool.

Wash and dry the spinach. Blanch in a large pot of salted boiling water. Shock in ice water to stop cooking. Drain and press any remaining water out of the leaves.

In a food processor, blend the cooked spinach with the cooled onion mixture. Add the chives, chervil and tarragon, and blend until smooth. Stir in cheeses, nutmeg, salt and freshly ground black pepper.

Make pasta dough and fill according to directions on page 173.

TOMATO COULIS: Heat the oil in a large pot over medium heat. Add onions, garlic, bay leaf and thyme; sweat for 5–7 minutes until soft and translucent. Add canned and fresh tomatoes and season with sugar, salt and freshly ground white pepper. Mix well, reduce heat to low, add basil and cook for 30–40 minutes until soft. Remove from heat and discard the herbs. Transfer to a blender or food processor and purée until smooth. Strain through fine-mesh sieve into clean pot. If coulis is too thick, add some of the reserved tomato juice. Keep warm until needed.

TO ASSEMBLE: Before serving, bring a large pot of salted water to a boil with 1 Tbsp. olive oil. Boil ravioli for 2–3 minutes. Drain well. Season with salt and freshly ground white pepper.

Melt butter in a large nonstick frying pan over medium-high heat. Quickly sauté the chanterelles, season with salt and freshly ground white pepper.

Warm the tomato coulis over medium heat and stir in a little olive oil. Season with salt and freshly ground white pepper.

To serve, divide chanterelles among 4 large bowls. Place ravioli on top of the chanterelles. Nap the coulis over the ravioli. Sprinkle on the Parmesan cheese. Drizzle some of the basil oil around the outside. Serve immediately.

WINE: A Beaujolais or a light simple red.

Serves 4

Herb ravioli with chanterelles,
tomato coulis and basil oil

Chanterelles with napa cabbage rolls and rosemary crème fraîche in a mushroom emulsion

CABBAGE ROLLS

1 large napa cabbage

1 Tbsp. olive oil

1 medium carrot, cut in medium dice

1 medium onion, thinly sliced

2 cups Israeli couscous, cooked
    (see page 106)

1 sprig rosemary leaves,
    chopped finely

1 cup crème fraîche

MUSHROOM EMULSION

1 cup mushroom stock (see page 170)

¼ cup white wine

1 Tbsp. heavy cream

5 Tbsp. unsalted butter

juice of ½ lemon

CHANTERELLES

1 Tbsp. olive oil

1 Tbsp. unsalted butter

½ lb. chanterelles, cleaned

2 Tbsp. chopped fine herbs, such as
    parsley, chives, chervil

garlic froth (see page 110) for garnish

1 bunch watercress, washed, dried
    and stemmed, for garnish

ABOUT THE RECIPE: This has been one of my most popular dishes on the vegetarian menu. The stuffing mix is made with Israeli couscous, which I love to use because of its wonderful texture. At the restaurant, we serve one roll per person as part of a tasting menu, but you may want to serve two if this will be a main dish.

I have no problem featuring the same ingredient more than once in a menu, especially during chanterelle season. To taste the same ingredient combined with different flavors and cooked using various techniques heightens the experience for me.

TO PREPARE CABBAGE ROLLS: Remove the larger outer leaves of the cabbage. Cut out and remove the thick cores of the leaves. Cut the cores and inner leaves of the cabbage into fine julienne; set aside. Bring a large pot of water to a boil and individually blanch the whole leaves until just tender. Immediately immerse the leaves in a bowl of ice water. Drain and set aside.

Heat oil in sauté pan over medium-high heat; add carrot and sweat until tender. Add cabbage julienne and onion. Season with salt and freshly ground white pepper. Sweat until tender. Remove from heat and allow to cool.

In a bowl, combine vegetables and cooked Israeli couscous. Stir in rosemary and crème fraîche. Adjust seasoning. Take one large cabbage leaf and place about ¼ cup of the vegetable and couscous mix in the middle of the leaf. Fold the bottom cored ends over the filling and fold sides of leaves over filling. Roll toward top part of the leaf to completely enclose filling. If the leaves are too small, you may need to overlap 2 leaves to enclose the filling. Reserve rolls fold-side down. Continue with the remaining leaves.

MUSHROOM EMULSION: In a small pot over medium heat, combine stock and wine and simmer to reduce by half. Add cream and gently whisk in the butter. Season with salt, freshly ground white pepper and lemon juice. Keep warm.

CHANTERELLES: Heat oil and butter in a large skillet over medium-high heat. Add chanterelles and sauté for 3–5 minutes. Pour any liquid into a small bowl and set aside. Continue cooking chanterelles until golden brown. Season with salt and freshly ground white pepper. Stir in finely chopped herbs. Strain chanterelle liquid into mushroom emulsion and add chanterelles. Keep warm.

TO ASSEMBLE: Cover the cabbage rolls lightly with plastic wrap and heat in a microwave for 1 minute or until heated through. Place 1 or 2 rolls in the center of each serving plate. Spoon mushroom emulsion and chanterelles over and around the cabbage rolls. If using garlic froth, foam it with a handheld blender and nap over rolls. Garnish with a small bouquet of watercress.

WINE: A good rich Pinot Noir, Burgundy or, more easily, a good '98 Côtes du Rhône.

Serves 4

Oysters on the half shell with tomato,
daikon and cucumber relish (facing)

Oysters on the half shell with tomato, daikon and cucumber relish

OYSTERS

24 small oysters

⅔ cup extra virgin olive oil

⅓ cup finely diced shallots

⅓ cup finely diced fennel

⅓ cup sherry vinegar

fine sea salt

RELISH

¼ cup finely diced tomato

¼ cup finely diced daikon

½ cup finely diced, peeled and
  seeded cucumber

¼ cup rice vinegar

3 Tbsp. mirin

1 tsp. granulated sugar

1 tsp. finely minced lemon zest

cilantro leaves, finely sliced

ABOUT THE RECIPE: This simple and elegant recipe is a great way to introduce oysters to those who aren't quite ready to eat them raw. On the West Coast we have a great variety of superb oysters to choose from, particularly in the colder months when they are much more flavorful. I particularly like to use Kumamoto oysters for this recipe.

TO PREPARE OYSTERS: Shuck the oysters. In a nonreactive dish, place the whole oysters in a single layer, cover with plastic wrap and refrigerate until ready to prepare. Discard the top shells and rinse and save the bottoms.

Heat ⅓ cup of the oil in a medium saucepan over medium heat. Add the shallots and fennel and sauté until softened, approximately 2 minutes. Stir in the remaining oil plus sherry vinegar, salt and freshly ground white pepper. Bring to a boil and pour over the raw oysters, spreading the shallots and fennel evenly over them. Let cool, then cover and refrigerate for 4 hours.

RELISH: Mix the tomatoes, daikon, cucumber, rice vinegar, mirin, sugar and zest and allow to sit 2–3 hours covered. Before serving, drain off excess liquid. Gently mix in cilantro and season.

TO ASSEMBLE: Just before serving, remove oysters from the marinade and place each oyster in one of the reserved shells. Reserve marinade. Spoon 1 tsp. of the relish over each oyster. Arrange 4–6 oysters on each serving plate. Sprinkle with some of the cilantro and serve immediately.

WINE: A crisp, simple white: a Muscadet, a light Sauvignon Blanc or a light and frisky Soave from Italy.

Serves 4 to 6

Seared scallops with baby leeks and blue cluster chanterelles in herb vinaigrette

1 cup blue cluster chanterelles
2 sprigs fresh thyme
1 large clove garlic, thinly sliced
1½ Tbsp. extra virgin olive oil
8 baby leeks or 1 large leek,
    white part only, cut in thin coins
1 Tbsp. grapeseed oil
4 large scallops, tendon removed

¼ cup house vinaigrette (see page 172)
1 tsp. fresh lemon juice
2 Tbsp. mixed chopped fresh herbs,
    such as tarragon, thyme, chervil,
    parsley, chives
1 cup mixed baby greens for garnish
lemon oil (see page 171) for garnish

ABOUT THE RECIPE: When you cook scallops and allow them to rest, the juices seep out. The great thing about this recipe is that you can add the vinaigrette to the scallop juices to warm it up, and include those succulent juices.

TO PREPARE: Preheat the oven to 400° F. Trim, separate and carefully clean chanterelles. Place in an ovenproof nonstick pan, sprinkle with thyme and garlic and drizzle the olive oil over. Roast uncovered in the oven for 10–15 minutes and set aside.

Bring a pot of salted water to a boil and blanch the leeks until tender, 4–6 minutes. Have a bowl of ice water on the side. Remove and plunge the leeks in the ice water.

In a second ovenproof nonstick skillet, heat grapeseed oil over medium-high heat. Season the scallops lightly with salt and freshly ground white pepper on each side. Place in hot pan and sear 1 side until golden brown. Turn scallops over, then place in oven. For medium rare, the scallops will take 2–3 minutes. Remove from oven and let the scallops rest in the pan for another 2–3 minutes. Keep warm.

Add the baby leeks to the chanterelles. Add the vinaigrette to the pan and gently heat.

To serve, lift chanterelles and leeks from pan with slotted spoon, reserving liquid. Divide chanterelle mixture among 4 plates. Place a scallop on top. Place scallop pan back on heat and deglaze it with 3 Tbsp. of the warmed vinaigrette from the chanterelle pan. Add lemon juice and quickly bring to a simmer. Remove from heat. Add fresh herbs. Season with salt and freshly ground white pepper. Pour scallop vinaigrette over and around the chanterelles and scallops.

Gently toss the baby greens with a small amount of lemon oil and place a bouquet of greens on top of scallops.

WINE: A nice earthy Chardonnay or Rhône Roussanne-based white.

Serves 4

*Seared spot prawns with puréed potatoes and
a lemon and tobiko beurre blanc (facing)*

Seared spot prawns with puréed potatoes and a lemon and tobiko beurre blanc

POTATO PURÉE

1¼ lbs. Yukon Gold potatoes, skins on

1 cup heavy cream, lukewarm

5 Tbsp. unsalted butter, cut in cubes

5 Tbsp. mascarpone cheese

½ tsp. sea salt

PRAWNS

12 spot prawns, 21–26 per pound or
    medium size

1½ Tbsp. vegetable oil

PHYLLO ROUNDS

1 sheet phyllo pastry

1 Tbsp. butter, melted

zest of 1 lemon

½ cup beurre blanc (see page 172)

1 Tbsp. tobiko (flying fish roe)

chickweed for garnish

ABOUT THE RECIPE: One of my favorite combinations is potato purée with fish. It's served often in Europe, particularly in Scandanavia, where potatoes are in everything. This recipe definitely appeals to the Irishman in me.

TO PREPARE POTATO PURÉE: Follow method on page 10.

PRAWNS: Season prawns on both sides with salt and freshly ground white pepper. Heat oil in a large nonstick skillet over medium-high heat. When hot, add the prawns to the pan and quickly sear both sides (about 1 minute per side). Remove and set aside.

PHYLLO ROUNDS: Preheat oven to 375° F. Take 1 sheet of phyllo pastry and cut it in half lengthwise. Brush one side with melted butter and place the other half on top. Transfer onto a parchment-lined baking sheet. Use a 3-inch round cutter to cut circles out of the phyllo. Brush the circles with melted butter and season with a little salt. Bake until they are lightly crisp, about 2–3 minutes. Remove from oven and cool.

TO ASSEMBLE: Stir lemon zest into the beurre blanc. Heat the beurre blanc very slightly. To serve, place potato purée in the middle of 4 individual soup plates. Sprinkle tobiko around the potatoes. Place the seared prawns on top of the purée. Drizzle warm beurre blanc over the tobiko circling the potato purée and prawns. Garnish with phyllo rounds and chickweed.

WINE: A nice Burgundy-style Chardonnay, rich but not sweetened with oak to excess.

Serves 4

Butter-braised Atlantic lobster with lobster bisque and mascarpone risotto

LOBSTER

2 qts. water

⅓ cup white wine vinegar

3 Tbsp. coarse sea salt or kosher salt

four 1-lb. lobsters

2½ cups beurre monté (see page 172)

LOBSTER BISQUE

⅓ cup grapeseed oil

2 lobster carcasses

1 cup finely chopped tomatoes

⅓ cup finely chopped carrots

⅓ cup finely chopped celery

⅓ cup finely chopped onion

4 sprigs tarragon

2 cups heavy cream

2 cups cooked mascarpone risotto
    (see page 174)

chopped chives for garnish

LOBSTER OIL

2 cups grapeseed oil

½ cup coarsely diced mixed carrot, onion,
    leek and celery

2 cloves garlic, crushed

2 sprigs thyme

1 lobster carcass, coarsely chopped

½ tsp. coarse salt

1 Tbsp. tomato paste

ABOUT THE RECIPE: This dish is not for the faint-hearted. In fact, it's just plain decadent. The velvety risotto is finished in lobster bisque and made extra creamy with the addition of cheese. The butter-braising makes the lobster so tender it will melt in your mouth.

I first learned this procedure several years ago when I was working at Emile Jung's Au Crocodile, a three-star restaurant in Strasbourg. Of all the three-star chefs in France, Chef Jung is probably the most classical in the way he prepares his sauces. I've also noticed that Thomas Keller, chef and owner of The French Laundry, uses a similar method to produce even-textured sauces. At Au Crocodile, beurre monté was the base for sauces and the base for poaching lobsters.

Poaching the live lobsters can be done ahead of time, which will give you the carcasses you need to prepare the lobster bisque and lobster oil.

TO PREPARE LOBSTER: Combine water, vinegar and salt and bring to a boil. Cook each lobster separately. Plunge the lobster into the boiling water and cook for 2 minutes. Do not overcook since the meat will undergo further cooking later. After 2 minutes, immerse in an ice bath and allow to rest.

Remove the meat from the tail and claw sections. Reserve the carcasses and use them for the lobster bisque.

LOBSTER BISQUE: Heat the oil in a large stockpot over medium heat. Put the lobster carcasses in the pot and cook over medium heat for 5–10 minutes until the lobster carcasses have turned dark red. Alternatively, place the lobster carcasses in a heavy roasting pan and drizzle the oil over them. Roast in a preheated 450° F oven for 5–10 minutes or until dark red. Transfer to a large stockpot.

Add the tomatoes, carrots, celery and onion and sauté over medium heat for 3–4 minutes. Add tarragon and just enough water to cover the shells. Bring to a simmer. Continue to simmer for 1 hour while skimming the foam off the top of the stock. Strain stock through a fine-mesh sieve, crushing lobster carcasses with a wooden spoon to extract as much liquid as possible. Once strained, place stock on stove and reduce by one-third. Add cream and reduce to approximately 3 cups of liquid. Season with salt and freshly ground white pepper.

LOBSTER OIL: In a large pot, heat 1 Tbsp. oil and add all the vegetables, garlic and thyme. Sweat for 3–4 minutes over medium-high heat, then add the chopped lobster carcass. Cook for another 2–3 minutes, then add salt, tomato paste and remaining oil, and simmer for 7–10 minutes. Remove from heat and let oil infuse for approximately 30 minutes. Strain liquid through a fine-mesh sieve or cheesecloth. Store refrigerated in an airtight container for up to 2 weeks.

TO ASSEMBLE: Before serving, place the beurre monté over medium heat. Do not boil as it will separate. Heat the rare lobster meat in the butter for 5–6 minutes until warmed through.

Place lobster bisque in a saucepan, bring to a simmer and reduce by half (you should have about 1¼ cups). Add the cooked risotto and season with salt and freshly ground white pepper. Let this simmer for 1–2 minutes. Remove from heat and keep warm.

To serve, divide the risotto among 4 serving plates. Remove the lobster meat from the beurre monté and arrange lobster meat on top of the risotto. Drizzle a little beurre monté over the lobster. Sprinkle with chives and a pinch of fleur de sel. Finish by drizzling lobster oil around the plate. Serve immediately.

WINE: A white Bordeaux or a big Chardonnay.

Serves 4 · photo, page 104

Butter-braised Atlantic lobster with lobster
bisque and mascarpone risotto (page 102)

Seared Arctic char with cauliflower purée and a smoked sablefish and horseradish emulsion

CAULIFLOWER PURÉE
1 medium head cauliflower
¼ cup heavy cream

EMULSION
1½ cups chicken stock (see page 169)
1 oz. smoked sablefish fillet
	(Alaska black cod)
1 Tbsp. creamed horseradish

1 Tbsp. unsalted butter
lemon juice, to taste

ARCTIC CHAR
four 2-oz. fillets, skin on, scaled
1 Tbsp. grapeseed oil

julienned flat-leaf parsley for garnish
fleur de sel for garnish

ABOUT THE RECIPE: Arctic char is one of my favorite fish. It's related to both salmon and trout. I usually use wild char, but the fish is farmed extensively so it's easy to get year round. It's a rich fish so it goes well with creamy, intense sauces.

The cauliflower purée is much lighter than a potato purée and I think it accents fish better.

TO PREPARE CAULIFLOWER PURÉE: Cut core out and separate cauliflower into florets. Blanch in a pot of boiling salted water until soft. Drain. Transfer to either food processor or blender and purée. Heat cream and add slowly to cauliflower until smooth. Strain through a fine-mesh sieve. Season with salt and freshly ground white pepper; set aside.

EMULSION: Bring stock to a boil. Simmer sablefish in stock for 2–3 minutes; remove from heat. Mash fish with a fork. Set fish aside for 5–10 minutes.

Strain liquid through a fine-mesh sieve. Reduce liquid by half and add horseradish. Add the mashed fish. Return to blender or food processor and purée again.

Place purée in pot over low heat and whisk in butter. Season with salt and freshly ground white pepper. Squeeze lemon juice into sauce. The sauce will keep warm for 5–10 minutes.

ARCTIC CHAR: Season both sides of fish with salt and freshly ground white pepper. Heat oil in a nonstick pan over medium heat. Place fish in pan skin-side down and sear until skin is crispy. Turn fish over, cook for 1 more minute and remove fish from pan. Keep fish warm.

TO ASSEMBLE: Place a few spoonfuls of the warm cauliflower purée in the center of 4 plates. Put a char fillet on top of purée and spoon emulsion around each. Garnish with parsley and fleur de sel.

WINE: A big rich Riesling or a balanced big Chardonnay.

Serves 4

Roasted duck with duck confit, Israeli couscous and a warm soy-ginger vinaigrette

DUCK CONFIT

2 cloves garlic, roughly chopped

2 bay leaves

2 Tbsp. coarse sea salt

3 Tbsp. black peppercorns, lightly cracked

4 sprigs thyme

3 duck legs with thighs attached

½ lb. rendered duck fat (or 1 lb. lard)

VINAIGRETTE

1 cup dark chicken stock (see page 169)

1 Tbsp. minced ginger

1 Tbsp. Japanese soy sauce

1 Tbsp. rice vinegar

juice of ½ lemon

COUSCOUS

1 cup Israeli couscous

1 Tbsp. grapeseed oil

1 Tbsp. unsalted butter

1 shallot, finely sliced

2 cups vegetable stock (see page 170)
    or five-spice duck consommé
    (see page 130)

DUCK BREASTS

1 Tbsp. extra virgin olive oil

4 large halves duck breast, skin on

extra virgin olive oil for garnish

1 cup mesclun greens for garnish

ABOUT THE RECIPE: I really enjoy combining two different cuts of the same thing in a dish. Here the duck leg and the breast, cooked in different ways, live happily with the warmth of a soy-ginger vinaigrette and the texture of Israeli couscous.

TO PREPARE DUCK CONFIT: Sprinkle the bottom of a roasting pan with 1 clove garlic, 1 bay leaf, 1 Tbsp. salt, 1½ Tbsp. peppercorns and 2 sprigs thyme. Arrange the duck legs in one layer in the bottom of the pan. Rub the seasonings onto the legs. Cover and refrigerate overnight.

Preheat the oven to 275° F. Rinse the duck legs in cold water and pat dry. In a saucepan over medium heat, melt the duck fat with remaining garlic, bay leaf, salt, peppercorns and thyme. Pour the fat over the legs, covering them completely. Cover the pan with aluminum foil and bake until the meat falls from the bone, about 2–3 hours. Tear the meat into small pieces if you are going to use it right away. Otherwise, the whole duck leg can be stored covered with the fat in the refrigerator for up to a month. Cover and refrigerate until needed.

VINAIGRETTE: In a saucepan over medium heat, combine stock and ginger; bring to a boil. Reduce heat and simmer for 10 minutes. Strain. Add soy sauce and vinegar. Season with salt and freshly ground white pepper to taste. Squeeze lemon juice into vinaigrette; set aside.

COUSCOUS: Preheat oven to 350° F. In a bowl, toss the couscous with the oil and spread onto a baking sheet. Bake until golden.

Melt butter in a medium saucepan over medium heat. Sweat the shallot until translucent. Add stock and bring to a boil. Add couscous, return to a boil, reduce heat and simmer covered until the couscous is soft. Stir occasionally. Sometimes the couscous will absorb all the stock before it is soft. If this happens, add a little more stock. Season with salt and freshly ground white pepper.

Serve immediately or spread couscous on a parchment-lined pan and allow to cool, then warm it up with a small amount of stock and unsalted butter.

DUCK BREASTS: Preheat oven to 475° F. Score the skin of the duck breasts to ensure even cooking. Season with salt and freshly ground pepper.

In a large ovenproof frying pan, heat the olive oil over high heat. Place seasoned breasts skin-side down and sear for 2–3 minutes. Pour fat from pan, place pan in the oven, and roast breasts for 5 minutes. Remove from oven and pour off remaining fat. Turn skin-side up and roast for a further 4–5 minutes for medium-rare. Remove from oven and keep warm on a rack, skin-side down.

TO ASSEMBLE: Heat 1 tsp. fat from the confit in a small saucepan over medium heat. Add 1 cup of the confit meat and heat for 1 minute. Add Israeli couscous and continue cooking for 2–3 minutes.

Slice each duck breast into 4 portions. On 4 large plates, place the couscous and confit mixture, add the sliced duck breasts on top, and drizzle warm soy-ginger vinaigrette over top. Finish with a drizzle of extra virgin olive oil around the duck. Top with a small bouquet of greens.

WINE: A rich Sangiovese or Chianti.

Serves 4

Blanching

Throughout this book you'll see vegetables and herbs being blanched separately before they're combined for final assembly, and although it may seem a bit painstaking to cook them once, then cook them again, it's worth it. The vegetables will turn a brilliant color and keep their crunch without sacrificing nutrients. And—big bonus—you can blanch things ahead of time and have them all ready so that the final preparations are stress free.

Blanching is simply parboiling vegetables or herbs, then cooling them as quickly as possible in an ice bath. Boiling times vary with each vegetable, which is why they all have to be blanched separately. If you want them just barely cooked, especially if they'll undergo further cooking, transfer them to an ice bath the minute the color brightens. If you want them slightly more cooked but still with some bite, watch them carefully once they turn brilliant and remove and cool them the moment you see any change in the color— probably a matter of less than a minute.

Remember that salt brings out both the color and the flavor, so don't forget to season the water. And have the water at a furious and consistent boil. This is not a gentle process—it's the shock of both the heat and the cold that makes blanching work.

< *Braised halibut casserole with wild mushrooms*
and black truffle butter (page 22)

Squab wrapped in potato with seared foie gras, squab jus and a garlic froth

SQUAB JUS

2 squabs, breasts removed
    and reserved
2 Tbsp. canola oil
¼ cup finely diced onions
¼ cup finely diced celery
¼ cup finely diced carrots
4 cloves garlic, crushed
4 cups dark chicken stock
    (see page 169)
3 sprigs thyme
4 Tbsp. unsalted butter

GARLIC FROTH

1 Tbsp. olive oil
5–8 cloves garlic
1½ tsp. honey
½ cup chicken stock (see page 169)
1 cup heavy cream
1 Tbsp. unsalted butter

SQUAB

breasts of 2 squabs
1 Tbsp. canola oil
2 cups large spinach leaves, de-stemmed
    and blanched
2 large Yukon Gold potatoes, peeled
    and passed through a Japanese turning
    slicer to form 4 long strings
canola oil for deep-frying

BEANS AND MUSHROOMS

1 cup thin green beans, blanched
1 cup thin wax beans, blanched
2 Tbsp. unsalted butter
½ lb. mixed mushrooms, cleaned
1 clove garlic, minced

FOIE GRAS

four 2-oz. pieces foie gras

ABOUT THE RECIPE: Outside of Hong Kong, Vancouver produces some of the best Asian food in the world and squab is a big part of the Chinese cuisine. Squab has the dark meat and assertive flavor of a game bird, and for some people it takes some getting used to. This preparation, a sublime combination of crispy potato on the outside, delicately soft squab breast on the inside and buttery foie gras, will win anyone over.

This might be the most complicated recipe in this cookbook, and it requires a very obscure piece of kitchen equipment, a Japanese turning slicer, which can cut vegetables into spaghetti-sized strings. But if you're willing to go to the trouble, you'll be rewarded.

TO PREPARE SQUAB JUS: Chop squab carcasses into small pieces. In a large sauté pan, heat canola oil over high heat. Add squab pieces and cook until very dark brown, stirring occasionally to prevent sticking. Reduce heat to medium-high and add onions, celery, carrots and garlic. Cook for 5 minutes, stirring occasionally.

Deglaze with stock, stirring up all the browned bits. Add thyme. Reduce liquid by half. Remove from heat and strain into a clean pot. Skim off all fat.

Over medium heat, reduce jus by one-third. Whisk in butter, a little at a time. Season with salt and keep warm.

GARLIC FROTH: Heat olive oil in small saucepan over medium-low heat. Gently sauté garlic until golden brown. Add honey and cook until garlic is caramelized, being careful not to burn it. Add stock and reduce until garlic is glazed and soft. Add ½ cup of the cream and bring to a boil. Reduce heat and simmer for 5 minutes. Remove from heat. Purée in blender or food processor and strain through fine-mesh sieve. Stir in butter.

In a small pot, bring remaining ½ cup cream to a boil. Add garlic purée and season with salt. Keep warm.

SQUAB: Score the skin on the squab breasts. Season both sides of the breasts with salt and freshly ground white pepper. Heat 1 Tbsp. canola oil in a large skillet, over high heat. Place seasoned squab breasts skin-side down and sear until skin becomes crispy; remove from pan. Allow squab breasts to cool. Wrap cooled breasts in blanched spinach leaves and wrap stringed potato around in a single layer.

Preheat oven to 400° F. In deep-fryer, heat canola oil to 325° F, or until a small piece of raw potato comes bubbling up to the surface when dropped in the oil. Deep-fry wrapped squab breasts for 3–4 minutes until potato is golden brown. Remove from pot and place on paper towels to absorb excess oil. Place squab breasts in a large ovenproof skillet and roast in oven for 2 minutes. Remove from oven and allow to rest.

BEANS AND MUSHROOMS: In a pot of boiling, salted water, blanch beans. Plunge in ice-cold water to stop cooking. Drain. Heat a sauté pan over medium-high heat, melt butter and add mushrooms and garlic. Cook until golden brown, stirring occasionally. Add beans and toss to warm.

FOIE GRAS: Score the foie gras on one side and season both sides with salt and freshly ground white pepper. In a large skillet over high heat, sear the seasoned foie gras with scored-side down for 1–1½ minutes on one side. Pour off fat and turn foie gras, making sure not to burn it. Cook for 1 minute on the other side. Remove from pan.

TO ASSEMBLE: Divide beans and mushrooms among 4 serving plates. Spoon squab jus over the beans. Place foie gras on beans and place squab breast on top or to the side. Froth warm garlic cream with a handheld blender and spoon over dish.

WINE: A big Pinot Noir from Côte de Nuits or Carneros.

Serves 4 · photo, page 149

Seared lamb loin with baekenofe

BAEKENOFE

3 cups chicken stock (see page 169)

4 sprigs thyme

3 cloves garlic, crushed

2 bay leaves

6 strips lean bacon, cut into ¼-inch pieces

2 Yukon Gold potatoes, peeled and cut
    in ½-inch dice

1 Tbsp. unsalted butter

1 Tbsp. olive oil

1 large onion, thinly sliced

1 carrot, peeled and sliced in
    ¼-inch coins

3 leeks, white part only, sliced
    ½-inch thick

½ cup white wine

LAMB

½ cup veal reduction (see page 167)

2 cups lamb stock (see page 168)

2 cloves garlic

2 sprigs thyme

1 Tbsp. unsalted butter

two 6-oz. lamb loins, trimmed and cleaned,
    trimmings reserved

3 Tbsp. canola oil

4 Tbsp. julienned flat-leaf parsley

fleur de sel or coarse sea salt for garnish

ABOUT THE RECIPE: In Alsace baekenofe is a Sunday vegetable and potato casserole made with meat marinated in Pinot Gris or other wine for a day before it's cooked. It was traditionally made in a very large clay baker, but most people didn't have an oven large enough to fit the dish in, so they would take it to the local baker who would bake it off for them, hence, baekenofe.

When I was working with Emile Jung in Strasbourg, he did the vegetables alone and served them in a mini clay baker with truffles.

TO PREPARE BAEKENOFE: Put 2 cups chicken stock in a medium pot and add 3 thyme sprigs, 1 garlic clove, 1 bay leaf, and ⅓ of the bacon. Add the potatoes, bring to a boil, reduce heat and simmer until cooked but still firm. Strain, reserving the stock. Remove thyme and bay leaf, and set aside potatoes.

Heat the butter and olive oil in a large saucepan over medium heat and sweat the remaining bacon. Add onions, carrots, remaining 2 garlic cloves, bay leaf and thyme sprig. Sweat uncovered for about 5 minutes. Add leeks and sweat uncovered a further 5 minutes.

Pour in the wine, stir and continue cooking for 3 minutes. Season with salt and freshly ground white pepper. Add the remaining 1 cup stock and cook another 5 minutes. When the vegetables are cooked, remove from liquid, discard bay leaf and thyme, and set aside.

Add reserved stock from the potatoes. Simmer the liquid until it is reduced by about half and has a syrupy consistency. Add cooked potatoes to the sauce and pour sauce over vegetables. Allow to cool and refrigerate until ready to use. Flavor will improve overnight.

LAMB: Preheat oven to 450° F. In a saucepan, combine the reduction, lamb stock, garlic and thyme. Bring to a boil and reduce by one-third. Strain into a clean pot through a fine-mesh sieve. Whisk in butter and adjust seasoning.

Season lamb loins with salt and freshly ground white pepper. Heat canola oil in a frying pan over medium-high heat. Add the lamb loins and sear on all sides until golden brown. Place in oven and cook to desired doneness. Remove from heat and allow to rest for 5–7 minutes, keeping warm.

TO ASSEMBLE: Before serving, reheat baekenofe over medium-low heat with a little butter to prevent sticking. Add parsley. Place a portion of baekenofe in the middle of each serving plate. Slice lamb loin ½-inch thick and place 1 portion in a fan on top of baekenofe. Spoon lamb sauce around outside of each serving. Sprinkle fleur de sel on top of the lamb.

WINE: A big rich Rhône Syrah; in a pinch an Aussie Shiraz, but it lacks the herbal notes for the baekenofe.

Serves 4

Braised sweetbreads with truffled green lentils

SWEETBREADS

½ lb. sweetbreads from milk-fed veal

3 slices bacon

¼ cup coarsely chopped carrot

1 stalk celery, coarsely chopped

½ onion, coarsely chopped

3 cloves garlic, minced

4 sprigs thyme

1 Tbsp. grapeseed oil

¼ cup veal reduction (see page 167)

SAUCE

¾ cup veal reduction (see page 167)

½ tsp. aged sherry vinegar

1 Tbsp. butter

1 tsp. fresh lemon juice

LENTILS

1 Tbsp. unsalted butter

3 strips double-smoked bacon

1 shallot, halved

1 carrot, quartered

1 leek, white part only, halved and cleaned

1 stalk celery, quartered

1 clove garlic, crushed

5 sprigs thyme, tied in bundle

1 bay leaf

1 cup green lentils, washed

2 cups chicken stock (see page 169)

1 Tbsp. unsalted butter

2 strips double-smoked bacon,
    finely diced

1 shallot, finely diced

½ cup veal reduction (see page 167)

1 tsp. chopped black truffles

truffle oil (optional)

2 tsp. thyme leaves

1 tsp. chopped flat-leaf parsley

1 tsp. finely chopped chives

2 tsp. chopped tarragon leaves

½ tsp. finely chopped rosemary

ABOUT THE RECIPE: Our veal sweetbreads in the Fraser Valley are exceptional. Veal is very limited in quantity here, but what there is, is wonderful. The braising technique lets the sweetbreads speak for themselves. Look for larger sweetbreads because the small ones are too difficult to clean.

As with all the recipes that call for black truffles, you can use truffle-infused oil or canned black truffles.

TO PREPARE SWEETBREADS: Soak sweetbreads in cold water and refrigerate overnight. Drain and rinse thoroughly with cold running water.

In a large saucepan over medium heat, sweat bacon. Add carrots, celery, onion and garlic; cook for 2–3 minutes until softened. Add thyme and sweetbreads. Add enough cold water to cover and bring to a boil. Remove from heat and allow to sit for 10 minutes.

Remove sweetbreads and transfer to a clean container. Strain liquid and cool. Pour over sweetbreads and refrigerate until ready to use.

Preheat oven to 400° F. Remove any membranes from the sweetbreads and cut the meat into 1-inch pieces. Season with salt and freshly ground white pepper. In a skillet, heat the oil over medium-high heat. When hot, add the sweetbreads and sear on all sides. Add reduction and transfer to oven for 5–7 minutes or until well glazed. Keep warm.

SAUCE: Heat reduction with vinegar in small pot over medium heat. Add butter and lemon juice and whisk to mix. Keep warm.

LENTILS: Melt butter in medium saucepan over medium heat. Add bacon, shallot, carrot, leek, celery and garlic with thyme and bay leaf. Cover pan and sweat vegetables for 5 minutes.

Add lentils and enough stock to cover. Simmer uncovered, checking often to make sure lentils are covered with stock. Keep adding stock as needed until lentils are cooked, about 20–30 minutes. Remove pot from heat. Take out and discard vegetables, herbs and bacon. Allow lentils to cool and refrigerate until ready to use.

To finish the lentils, heat 1 tsp. of the butter in a large pan over medium heat. Sweat bacon and shallot until transparent. Add reduction and lentils. Cook until lentils are warmed through. Add truffles and a few drops of truffle oil. Whisk in the remaining 2 tsp. butter. Season to taste with salt and freshly ground white pepper. Add mixed herbs and keep warm.

TO ASSEMBLE: Place a mound of truffled lentils in center of 4 plates. Place sweetbreads on truffles. Spoon warmed sauce on top and around the dish.

WINE: A good Riesling.

Serves 4

Apple galette with fennel ice cream (page 162)

Selles-sur-Cher cheese with quince jelly

2 cups white wine
½ stick cinnamon
pulp of ½ pod vanilla

2 ¼ lb. quince, coarsely chopped
granulated sugar
four 1-oz. portions Selles-sur-Cher cheese

ABOUT THE RECIPE: This is a seriously aged goat cheese. The quince jelly cuts
the sharpness.

TO PREPARE: In a heavy pot, simmer wine with cinnamon stick. Reduce by one-third.
Add vanilla and chopped quince. Cook until quince is soft. Remove cinnamon stick.
Purée and pass through a fine-mesh sieve. For every ⅔ cup of purée, measure ½ cup sugar.
Place purée and sugar in a clean pot and simmer, stirring constantly. When a spoon leaves a
trail when passed through the mixture, pour jelly into a sterile glass container. Allow it to
cool and set, about 30 minutes.

To serve, place cheese on a plate with a spoonful of quince jelly.

WINE: A crisp Sancerre or Sauvignon Blanc from a cool climate.

Serves 4, with leftover quince jelly

Epoisses de Bourgogne cheese with macerated fruit

1 cup assorted dried fruits, such as
   currants, cranberries, figs
¼ cup port
2 Tbsp. apple juice
juice of 1 lemon

½ cup port wine
½ cup balsamic vinegar
four 1-oz. portions Epoisses de
   Bourgogne cheese

ABOUT THE RECIPE: This is a strong-smelling cheese that is washed with marc, the
French equivalent of grappa. It can stand up to poached dried fruits.

TO PREPARE: Combine fruits, port, apple juice and lemon juice in a pot over medium
heat. Cover and simmer for about 10 minutes until fruit is rehydrated.

Combine port and vinegar in a small pot over medium heat and reduce to a syrup.

To serve, divide fruit among 4 individual serving plates. Place cheese on top. Garnish
plate with port wine reduction.

WINE: A rich Sauvignon Blanc or a Sauternes-style dessert wine; good too with Marc
de Bourgogne.

Serves 4

Beaufort cheese with poached figs

1½ cups port wine
½ cup water
3 Tbsp. sugar
juice of 2 lemons
4 fresh figs
four 1-oz. portions Beaufort cheese

ABOUT THE RECIPE: This Savoie cow's milk cheese tastes like a well-aged Gruyère. The mild sweetness of figs is a perfect complement.

TO PREPARE: In a saucepan, bring the port, water, sugar and lemon juice to a boil. Add figs, reduce heat and simmer for 3 minutes. Remove saucepan from heat and allow figs to cool in liquid. Refrigerate overnight, covered, keeping figs in liquid until ready to use.

Before serving, remove figs from liquid. In a small pot, simmer liquid until it coats the back of a spoon. Stir occasionally during reduction to prevent burning.

To assemble, place a fig on each serving plate and cut in half. Drizzle with port wine reduction. Place cheese on the side.

WINE: A light tawny port; without figs, a crisp Chablis.

Serves 4

Spice cake with espresso dark rum ice cream

ICE CREAM

1 cup heavy cream

1 cup milk

¼ cup ground espresso beans

4 egg yolks

¼ cup + 2 Tbsp. sugar

2 Tbsp. dark rum

SPICE CAKE

2 cups all-purpose flour

1 tsp. baking soda

½ tsp. ground cinnamon

¼ tsp. ground cloves

¼ tsp. ground nutmeg

¾ cup unsalted butter

¾ cup brown sugar

1 egg

1 cup buttermilk

1 cup raisins

ABOUT THE RECIPE: Thank you, Mom. I grew up on this cake. It only ever lasted about an hour after it came out of the oven. Whenever Mom's in the restaurant and this is on the menu, she loves to go around to all the tables and let everyone know it's her recipe.

TO PREPARE ICE CREAM: In a heavy pot, bring cream, milk and ground espresso to a boil. Remove from heat. In a stainless steel bowl, whisk yolks and sugar; temper with one-third of the warmed cream mixture. Pour remaining cream into yolk mixture and place over boiling water. Cook, stirring, until mixture thickens and reaches 180° F. Add dark rum. Cool and refrigerate overnight.

Strain through a fine-mesh sieve. Place in ice cream maker and process according to manufacturer's directions.

SPICE CAKE: Preheat oven to 350° F. Butter and flour six 3-inch ramekins or muffin cups. Sift flour, baking soda and spices into a bowl. Using an electric mixer, cream butter in a separate bowl until soft. With mixer still running, slowly add the sugar and beat until fluffy. Add egg and beat well. Alternately add dry ingredients and buttermilk to the batter in 3 stages, mixing well after each addition. Fold in raisins. Pour into prepared ramekins or pans.

Bake 30–40 minutes, or until lightly browned and a toothpick comes out clean. Remove the ramekins or pan to a wire rack and cool completely. Turn the cakes out.

TO ASSEMBLE: Serve cake with a small scoop of ice cream on top.

WINE: Vin Santo or a Mediterranean Passito-style wine.

Serves 6

Building a menu

I'm continually trying to expand my horizons. Traveling around—
seeing what other people are doing, learning why they're doing
it and finding new products—really inspires me with new ideas for
surprising and satisfying the palate.

The best dishes have a sense of spontaneity. When I come up
with a new dish, I don't like to think about it too much, otherwise it
becomes contrived. I just try with each ingredient to bring out the
clear, natural flavor rather than masking it with a lot of other tastes.
A good piece of meat or fish doesn't need much done to it—it's the
garnishes, sauces and accompaniments that add the play of sour-salty-
sweet, hot-cold, liquid-solid or crunchy-creamy. If someone says
"I can taste everything on my plate," I'm happy. Then, for contrast,
I occasionally like to throw in a mystery flavor to make people think.

In building a menu, I follow a basic arc from lighter to heavier,
but within that structure are infinite possibilities.

My first rule is, if it's in season use it. If it's a particularly inspir-
ing ingredient, I may use it a couple of times in different contexts
so that the repetition itself becomes an extra element of the meal.
But I don't repeat treatments. Each dish in the menu has to come
from a new angle and use the building blocks in a distinct way so that
the meal leads the diner on an exploration that stimulates a particular
combination of senses with each course.

I want each meal to be an adventure. I want it to be art.

< Passion fruit tart with a dark
Valrhona chocolate base (page 158)

Fig tatin with Sambuca ice cream

ICE CREAM

1 cup whole milk

1 cup heavy cream

5 egg yolks

¼ cup sugar

2 Tbsp. Sambuca or anise-flavored
   liqueur

FIG TATIN

four 5-inch circles fresh puff pastry
   or 1 package thawed frozen puff pastry

12 fresh figs

¼ cup Sambuca or anise-flavored
   liqueur

ABOUT THE RECIPE: This is a spin-off of the famed French upside-down apple tart, *tarte tatin*, but it's made with fresh figs. The anise-flavored ice cream heightens the caramelization of the figs and the pastry crust.

TO PREPARE ICE CREAM: In a saucepan over medium heat, bring milk and cream to a boil. In a bowl, whisk yolks and sugar to a light-ribbon stage. Slowly add cream and milk to yolk mixture. Cook in a water bath until thickened, or until mixture coats the back of a metal spoon. Cool. Stir in Sambuca. Cover and refrigerate overnight.

Place in ice cream machine and churn according to directions. When ready, transfer to an airtight container and keep frozen.

FIG TATIN: Roll out puff pastry dough to ¼-inch thickness. Cut into 5-inch circles— or, if you will be making it in one pan, a 9-inch circle. The dough will shrink, so the circles should be slightly bigger than whatever they will be cooked in. Place the pastry on a parchment-lined baking sheet. Prick dough with fork, cover with plastic wrap and transfer tray to freezer to chill. Remove when ready to use.

Preheat the oven to 400° F. Quarter figs lengthwise. Toss with Sambuca. Butter and sugar four 4-inch ramekins or one 8-inch springform pan. Arrange the figs skin-side down in a fan. Place a frozen puff pastry circle on top of each ramekin. Bake for 10 minutes or until the puff pastry is golden.

TO ASSEMBLE: Let the tatin cool down for a few minutes before inverting onto a serving plate. Serve immediately with Sambuca ice cream.

WINE: A tawny Port, Pedro Ximenez or, in a perfect world, a Mavrodaphne of Patras.

Serves 4

Warm chocolate cake with sweet corn ice cream

ICE CREAM

5 ears sweet corn

2 Tbsp. coconut milk

¾ cups + 2 Tbsp. whole milk

¾–1 cup sugar (depending on how
  sweet the corn is)

1 cup heavy cream

5 egg yolks

CHOCOLATE CAKE

¼ lb. unsalted butter (½ cup), plus
  some for molds

4 oz. bittersweet chocolate,
  preferably Valhrona

2 large eggs

2 large egg yolks

¼ cup granulated sugar

3 tsp. flour, plus some for molds

ABOUT THE RECIPE: Who would think of making an ice cream with corn? Because of the sweetness of the local Peaches-and-Cream corn it works amazingly well.

TO PREPARE ICE CREAM: Cut corn kernels from cobs with sharp knife. Cook kernels with coconut milk, whole milk and half the sugar. Gently simmer uncovered until corn is tender.

Purée corn in blender. Press purée gently in a fine-mesh sieve to release as much liquid as possible. Combine purée with cream in a pot and bring to a boil over medium heat. Remove from heat.

Whisk remaining sugar with egg yolks until incorporated. Pour a small amount of the cream mixture into eggs to temper. Add remaining cream mixture and stir to incorporate. Pour mixture into a double boiler over simmering water and stir continuously. When mixture has thickened, remove from heat and cool in an ice bath to stop cooking.

Cover and refrigerate overnight. Strain once more and process in an ice cream machine according to the manufacturer's instructions.

CHOCOLATE CAKE: Butter and flour eight 3-inch molds, custard cups or ramekins. In the top of a double boiler set over simmering water, melt the butter and chocolate together and mix well. Remove from heat.

Combine eggs, yolks and sugar in a stainless steel bowl or double boiler over simmering water. With an electric mixer, beat egg mixture until doubled in volume. Remove from heat. (The gentle heat gives more volume to the mixture.)

When chocolate mixture is partially cooled, fold ⅓ of egg mixture into chocolate. iAdd remaining egg mixture to chocolate. Sift ½ of flour into mixture. Fold eggs and flour into chocolate, sift in remaining flour and continue folding until incorporated.

Divide the batter among the molds, filling each one no more than ¾ full. Refrigerate for at least 1 hour.

Preheat the oven to 375° F. Place ramekins on baking sheet and bake for 8–10 minutes. Cakes are done when the top is uniformly colored and slightly puffed.

TO ASSEMBLE: Remove from the oven and let set for 3–5 minutes before unmolding onto serving plates. Place a scoop of ice cream on the side. Serve immediately.

WINE: Banyuls Vin Doux Naturel.

Serves 8 · photo, page 73

{ W I N T E R }

VANCOUVER WINTERS are gray. We're used to it. Mostly the locals stay indoors avoid-

ing the drizzle. These months are for feeding the soul. We have to offer glorious hearty

food, so we braise and we glaze. Give me roasted meat on the bone—wild game, maybe—

with big juicy red wines. And oysters: December is the best time to eat them, plump and

sea-tasting, fresh from the cold waters to the northwest. Fabulous seasonal cheeses appear

from France. Parmesan-rich risottos and pastas seem to call. I have to have warm desserts,

like an apple galette or a big soufflé. Citrus, spices, butter, caviar and a nice roast chicken

are what the body craves. Why fight it?

I love to elaborate on all these theme foods of winter. The elements are rich and heavy

by nature, but as part of a menu with contrasting notes of color and tartness, each small

course satisfies the body and the senses without the full feeling that comes from overeating.

VEGETARIAN MENU

Warm endive and blood-orange salad
with Roquefort cheese and walnuts   *133*

Puréed celeriac soup with braised
salsify, chopped chestnuts and a red wine
and beet emulsion   *128*

Cassoulet of beans with a red wine
and mushroom emulsion   *139*

Pumpkin gnocchi with baby bok choy
and a mushroom consommé   *137*

Sainte Maure de Touraine cheese
with dates   *154*

Apple sorbet with spiced
apple jus   *175, 179*

Passion fruit tart with a dark
Valrhona chocolate base   *158*

SIGNATURE MENU

Warm Yukon Gold blinis with
osetra caviar   *138*

Five-spice duck consommé with duck
confit and caramelized onion ravioli   *130*

Seared Alaskan scallops with
a saffron-vanilla cream   *140*

Seared halibut with a kumquat and
cumin beurre blanc   *147*

Poulet rôti à la grand-mère   *148*

Pancetta-wrapped rabbit loin with
couscous in a squab jus   *153*

Côte de boeuf and braised short ribs with
a celeriac purée   *150*

Roquefort cheese with caramelized
pears and cilantro   *154*

Tangerine sorbet with
hibiscus jus   *176, 179*

Walnut cake with maple ice cream   *161*

SEAFOOD MENU

Poached smoked sablefish salad
with baby wild greens, Rose potatoes
and a horseradish and grainy
mustard vinaigrette   *134*

Seared Alaskan scallops and poached
Pearl Bay oysters with a hijiki and
soy-ginger broth   *145*

Butter-braised Atlantic lobster
with leek ravioli and a red beet and
horseradish sauce   *142*

Skate wings with a browned
butter sauce   *146*

Fourme d'Ambert cheese with
candied walnuts   *155*

Lemon sorbet with
lavender jus   *176, 179*

Apple galette with fennel
ice cream   *162*

Puréed celeriac soup with braised salsify, chopped chestnuts and a red wine and beet emulsion

6 fresh chestnuts (optional)

SALSIFY
½ lemon
3 stalks salsify
1 cup vegetable stock (see page 170)
1 Tbsp. unsalted butter

EMULSION
1 medium red beet
¾ cup dry red wine
¼ cup vegetable stock (see page 170)
2 Tbsp. heavy cream
2 Tbsp. unsalted butter

CELERIAC SOUP
2 Tbsp. olive oil
1 large celeriac, peeled and
    coarsely chopped
⅓ medium onion, thinly sliced
2 stalks celery, sliced
1 clove garlic
1 bay leaf
1 sprig thyme
1 cup dry white wine
4 cups vegetable or chicken stock
    (see page 170 or 169)
2 cups heavy cream

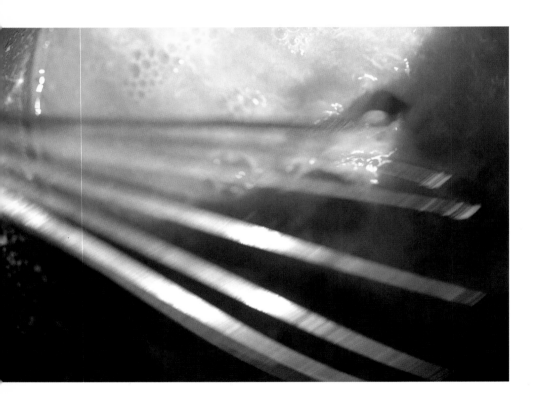

ABOUT THE RECIPE: This spectacular soup encompasses the intense flavor of celeriac. It's best on the same day it's made, as are all puréed soups.

Salsify, also called oyster plant, is a very good match for celeriac. It's very delicate, with almost a vanilla tone to the taste. Braised salsify would be good with scallops too. Unfortunately salsify is not easy to find. Try natural food stores or farmers' markets between October and March. You may have more luck finding burdock root, which can often be found in Asian markets. The cooking method is identical. Celeriac and salsify oxidize very quickly so you have to have acidulated water on hand as you're cutting them.

TO PREPARE CHESTNUTS: Preheat oven to 375° F. Slit the skins of the chestnuts and place chestnuts on a foil-lined baking sheet. Bake for 25–35 minutes. Remove and cool. Peel, coarsely chop and set aside.

SALSIFY: Squeeze lemon juice into a bowl of cold water. Peel salsify and cut into 1-inch rounds. Immediately place in lemon water to prevent oxidation.

In a saucepan, place stock, butter, salsify and a pinch of salt. Bring to a light boil over medium heat. Reduce heat and simmer until salsify is tender, about 5–10 minutes. Remove salsify, and set aside, reserving liquid.

Reduce liquid to a syrup. Add salsify and stir until it is glazed. Set aside.

EMULSION: Trim greens off beet, leaving ½ inch of stem attached. In a pot, place beet and enough water to cover. Bring to a boil, then simmer uncovered until beet is fork tender. Remove beet from water and allow to cool. When beet is cool enough to handle, peel and roughly chop.

Combine beet, red wine and stock in pot and simmer for 5 minutes. Transfer to blender or food processor and purée. Press through a fine-mesh sieve. Combine purée and cream in a pot and bring to a light simmer over medium heat. Whisk in butter and season with salt. Remove from heat and set aside.

CELERIAC SOUP: Heat the oil in a large saucepan over medium heat. Add celeriac, onion, celery, garlic, bay leaf and thyme; sauté until soft. Deglaze with white wine and reduce until liquid is evaporated. Add the stock; simmer for 10 minutes.

Add cream and bring to a boil. Season with salt and freshly ground white pepper. Remove thyme and bay leaf. Purée mixture in a blender and pass through a fine-mesh sieve.

TO ASSEMBLE: Place a little salsify in each bowl. Ladle 1 cup of soup into each bowl and drizzle with emulsion. Garnish with chopped chestnuts.

WINE: A big Bordeaux or California Cabernet.

Serves 4

Five-spice duck consommé with
duck confit and caramelized onion ravioli

CONSOMMÉ

¼ cup vegetable oil

¼ cup coarsely chopped carrots

¼ cup coarsely chopped celery

¼ cup coarsely chopped onions

¼ cup coarsely chopped fennel

4 cloves garlic, crushed

2 Tbsp. coarsely chopped ginger

1 Tbsp. coarsely chopped lemon grass

1 medium tomato, coarsely chopped

¼ cup soy sauce

¼ cup rice vinegar

1 whole Chinese barbecued duck,
cut into small pieces (available at
Asian markets)

2–3 qts. cold water or chicken stock
(see page 169)

3–4 sprigs flat-leaf parsley

4 sprigs thyme

½ cup finely chopped mixed carrots,
onions, leeks and celery

1 small tomato, finely chopped

3 egg whites

RAVIOLI

1 Tbsp. vegetable oil

2 Tbsp. duck fat (from confit)

2 medium finely chopped onions

5 sprigs thyme, bundled

pinch of sea salt

½ cup duck confit meat (see page 106)

2 cloves garlic, minced

¼ recipe pasta dough (see page 173)

white truffle oil for garnish

ABOUT THE RECIPE: I get crispy Peking duck in Chinatown and make the duck stock for the consommé. It's a great way to showcase the Asian flavors of Vancouver. When you buy the barbecued duck, ask the butcher to give you all the juice that's inside. That's where the flavor of the spices comes from.

TO PREPARE CONSOMMÉ: Heat the oil in a large stockpot over medium heat. Add carrots, celery, onions, fennel, garlic, ginger, lemon grass and tomato and sweat, stirring occasionally until vegetables start to brown.

Deglaze pan with soy sauce and vinegar. Add the duck pieces and any juice from the duck cavity. Sweat the duck pieces for 2–3 minutes. Pour in enough water or stock to cover. Add parsley and thyme and bring to a boil uncovered. Reduce heat and simmer for 1 to 1½ hours. Strain the liquid through a sieve and cool completely.

In a stainless steel bowl, combine the ½ cup mixed vegetables, tomato and egg whites. Gradually mix together and slowly whisk to a light foam.

Ensure that the duck stock is completely cool before continuing. This process of clarifying the consommé only works with cold stock. Skim and discard all fat. Place the cold stock in a large saucepan, slowly stir in the egg mixture and place over medium to low heat; bring to a simmer. Once it comes to a simmer, stop stirring.

The mixture that will form at the top of the simmering consommé is called a raft. You will notice that when you simmer it very slightly, a hole will start to emerge in the center. For the clarification to work, bring this mixture to a light simmer only, and do not boil. If the stock boils, the raft will separate and will make the consommé cloudy. Simmer 20–30 minutes.

Through the hole in the raft, gradually ladle 2–3 ounces of consommé at a time through a cheesecloth-lined chinois or a fine-mesh sieve. (Do not strain or break up the raft mixture.) Do this until the liquid is completely clear.

RAVIOLI: In a large pot on medium heat, combine oil and duck fat. When hot, add the onions, thyme and salt. Allow to sweat. When onions are transparent, increase heat and stir with a wooden spoon until onions caramelize, scraping bottom to prevent burning.

When the onions are dark brown, remove from heat and set aside to cool. Remove thyme bundle. Finely chop duck meat and onions together. Add garlic. For a finer filling, process in a food processor until smoother. Adjust seasoning.

Roll pasta dough and make into ravioli (see page 173).

TO ASSEMBLE: Heat the consommé slightly and season it with salt. In each of 4 bowls, place the ravioli. Pour the consommé over the ravioli. Serve immediately.

WINE: A medium sherry.

Serves 4 · photo, page 84

Baby greens salad with goat cheese, walnuts, shaved
Parmesan and a honey-blossom vinaigrette (page 90)

Warm endive and blood-orange salad with Roquefort cheese and walnuts

4 whole Belgian endives

2 Tbsp. grapeseed oil

3 tsp. sugar

2 Tbsp. water

1½ cups blood-orange juice

1 Tbsp. lemon juice, or to taste

4 medium blood oranges

¼ cup fresh Roquefort cheese

⅓ cup walnut halves, toasted

1 Tbsp. extra virgin olive oil

ABOUT THE RECIPE: This is one of my favorite salads and it appears often as part of the vegetarian menu. The caramelization of the slightly bitter endives blends well with the contrasting sweet acidity of the blood oranges and the Roquefort.

Blood oranges have a smooth or pitted skin sometimes blushed with red. They appear around December and sometimes are available until June. Look for Moro, a California variety that has rich burgundy fruit and a wonderful orange-raspberry taste.

TO PREPARE: Cut each of the Belgian endives in half lengthwise and remove the core. Heat grapeseed oil in a large nonstick frying pan over medium-high heat. When it is hot, add the endives to the pan and sear them on both sides. Add the sugar and cook until the endives are golden and have caramelized. Reduce heat to medium-low, add water and cover. Cook the endives until fork tender, 10–12 minutes. Remove from heat and set aside to cool. The endives may be cut in half again for serving or left as is.

For the dressing, add the blood-orange juice to a small saucepan and bring to a boil. Then turn down heat and slowly simmer, stirring occasionally. Reduce the juice until it becomes a syrup. Don't let it reduce too far or the natural sugar will caramelize and burn. Remove from heat and set aside. When syrup has cooled, whisk in the lemon juice. Season with salt and freshly ground white pepper.

TO ASSEMBLE: Peel the oranges, removing as much of the pith as possible, and cut evenly into ¼-inch rounds; you should get 3–4 slices from each orange. Overlap orange slices evenly in a circle on each of 4 plates.

On a separate plate, drizzle a bit of the blood-orange jus over the endives, cover and microwave to warm up (depending on the microwave, 20–30 seconds).

Place the endives on top of the orange slices. Crumble some Roquefort on top of each salad and arrange the walnuts around the outsides of the plates. Drizzle some blood-orange jus over the salads and some olive oil around the plates.

WINE: A Viognier or an off-dry Chenin Blanc.

Serves 4 · photo, page 88

Poached smoked sablefish salad with baby wild greens, Rose potatoes and a horseradish and grainy mustard vinaigrette

POTATOES

8 whole baby Rose potatoes
 or 1 large Yukon Gold potato,
 peeled and diced (1 cup)
½ tsp. sea salt
1 cup chicken stock (see page 169)

VINAIGRETTE

1½ tsp. grainy mustard
1 tsp. Dijon mustard
4 Tbsp. red wine vinegar
4 Tbsp. creamed horseradish
1½ tsp. lemon juice
½ cup grapeseed oil

SABLEFISH

1 cup whole milk
¼ cup water
2 sprigs thyme
1 bay leaf
1 clove garlic, lightly smashed
four 2-oz. portions smoked
 sablefish, skinless

GREENS

1 large leek, white and light green part only
2 cups mixed baby greens, such as arugula,
 chickweed or mizuna
¼ medium red onion, thinly sliced
2 radishes, thinly sliced

caviar for garnish (optional)

ABOUT THE RECIPE: Of all the dishes in the restaurant, this sums up Canadian cuisine for me. It's a Feenie family recipe made more elegant with a few additions.

Everybody's big on sablefish now, but I grew up on it. My dad was a fireman who used to cook a lot at home, and one of the things he loved was smoked black Alaska cod, which is what it was called back then. We used to have it at least once a month, poached in milk and served with potatoes.

For the restaurant, we get naturally smoked sablefish from the local fishermen.

TO PREPARE POTATOES: In a medium saucepan, bring potatoes, salt and stock to a boil. Reduce heat and simmer for 4–5 minutes or until potatoes are fork tender. Remove potatoes from stock and allow to cool. Reduce stock until syrupy.

For baby potatoes, cut in half. Mix potatoes with reduced stock.

VINAIGRETTE: In a small bowl, combine the mustards, vinegar, horseradish and lemon juice. Mix ingredients with a handheld blender, and slowly drizzle in oil until emulsified. This vinaigrette separates easily, so you may need to blend again before serving.

SABLEFISH: In a medium saucepan, bring the milk, water, thyme, bay leaf and garlic just to a boil. Turn heat to low and place fish in liquid. Poach fish in liquid for 4–5 minutes. Remove from heat and keep warm.

GREENS: Bring a pot of salted water to a boil. Cut leek into ½-inch rounds and rinse well. Blanch in boiling water 3–5 minutes until leek is tender. Plunge into ice water to stop cooking. Drain.

TO ASSEMBLE: Place potatoes and leeks on 1 plate with 2 Tbsp. of the vinaigrette. Season with salt and freshly ground white pepper. Warm in microwave for 20 seconds.

In a small bowl, toss the baby greens, onion and radishes with enough vinaigrette to coat. (The remaining vinaigrette can be stored in a sealed jar.) Season with salt and freshly ground white pepper.

To serve, divide warmed potatoes and leeks among 4 plates. Top with dressed salad greens and place 1 portion warm sablefish on top of salad. For an elegant touch, garnish fish with a spoonful of caviar. Serve immediately.

WINE: A spicy Alsace Riesling.

Serves 4 · photo, page 152

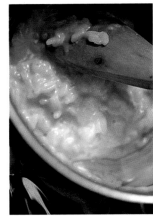

Pumpkin gnocchi with baby bok choy
and a mushroom consommé (facing)

Pumpkin gnocchi with baby bok choy and a mushroom consommé

GNOCCHI

1 small sweet pumpkin

vegetable oil

2 lbs. Yukon Gold potatoes, skins on

3 egg yolks

1½ cups sifted flour

¼ tsp. salt

¼ tsp. ground nutmeg

BOK CHOY

8 baby bok choy, trimmed and washed

1 Tbsp. unsalted butter

2 cups mushroom consommé (see page 13)

toasted pumpkin seeds for garnish

pumpkin seed oil for garnish (available at Middle Eastern and specialty stores)

ABOUT THE RECIPE: I love gnocchi and they're one of the easiest things to make. They're simply potato dumplings, to which you can add any flavor you like. The basic gnocchi recipe (see page 173) we have is foolproof. The secret is to make sure the dough isn't too sticky—it needs just enough flour to absorb most of the moisture.

TO PREPARE GNOCCHI: Preheat oven to 400° F. Cut pumpkin in half lengthwise and remove stem and seeds. Coat with a small amount of oil. Season with salt and freshly ground white pepper. Place cut-side down on baking sheet and roast until soft, about 1 hour. Allow to cool.

Scrape pumpkin flesh from skin. Purée pumpkin in food processor and press through a fine-mesh sieve. Retain 1 cup purée for gnocchi. Any extra can be frozen in resealable plastic bags and used for another purpose.

In a pot, cover potatoes with salted water, bring to a boil and simmer until fork tender. Drain. When cool enough to handle, remove skins. Pass potatoes through a ricer into a large bowl.

Combine potato, pumpkin purée and yolks until smooth. In a separate bowl, combine flour, salt and nutmeg and add freshly ground white pepper to taste. Slowly add dry ingredients to potato mixture. Knead until smooth. Continue as for gnocchi on page 173.

BOK CHOY: Blanch bok choy in a pot of boiling salted water for 2 minutes. Immediately plunge into ice water to stop cooking. Drain and dry on paper towels.

Melt butter in nonstick skillet over medium heat. Add bok choy and season with salt and freshly ground white pepper. Sauté until warmed through.

TO ASSEMBLE: Heat consommé and adjust seasonings. Rewarm gnocchi in consommé. In each of 4 serving bowls place ¼ cup consommé and some gnocchi. Place two bok choy on top. Garnish with pumpkin seeds and drizzle pumpkin seed oil around the consommé.

WINE: A light and lovely Pinot Noir.

Serves 4

Warm Yukon Gold blinis
with osetra caviar

1 lb. Yukon Gold potatoes, skins on
2 Tbsp. all-purpose flour
1 Tbsp. crème fraîche
2 large eggs
1 large egg yolk

GARNISHES
1 oz. beluga or osetra caviar
2 Tbsp. crème fraîche
1 Tbsp. capers, finely chopped
1 large egg, hard-boiled, chopped
1 shallot, peeled and finely diced
   or ⅓ medium onion, finely diced

ABOUT THE RECIPE: This easy-to-follow recipe is foolproof. It makes a very elegant dish that can be served on its own or with caviar or other accompaniments.

I prefer Yukon Golds because of their sweetness and creamy texture. For me, these potatoes are like my knives: I feel comfortable working with them. They're a great Canadian potato.

TO PREPARE: Place the potatoes in salted water, bring to a boil and simmer, covered, until thoroughly cooked. Drain and, while the potatoes are still warm, peel them and press through a fine-mesh sieve or ricer. Quickly work in the flour with a fork or spoon and mix in the crème fraîche. Add one egg and mix in until the batter is smooth. Add the second egg and then the yolk, mixing well after each addition. Season with salt and freshly ground white pepper. The batter should have the texture of a pancake batter. If necessary, add a bit more crème fraîche to reach the right consistency.

Preheat a nonstick pan over medium heat until very hot. Spoon about 1½ tsp. of the batter into the pan. Cook until the bottom is golden brown, 2–3 minutes, turn and cook the other side for a further minute. Place cooked blinis on a small baking sheet and keep warm.

To serve, place a small dollop of caviar on the blini and garnish with crème fraîche. Serve with capers, chopped egg and chopped shallots on the side. Never use lemon as a garnish with caviar as the acidity will overpower the delicate flavor of the caviar.

WINE: Champagne, champagne or champagne.

Serves 4 · photo, page 144

Cassoulet of beans with a red wine and mushroom emulsion

DRIED BEANS

2 Tbsp. dried navy beans, soaked
   overnight in 1 cup water
2 Tbsp. dried cranberry beans, soaked
   overnight separately in 1 cup water
1 cup vegetable or chicken stock
   (see page 170 or 169)
one 2-inch piece leek, cut in half lengthwise
one 2-inch piece carrot, cut in half
   lengthwise
½ medium onion, cut in half lengthwise

EMULSION

½ cup mushroom stock (see page 170)
⅓ cup red wine
1 Tbsp. unsalted butter

CASSOULET

1 tsp. unsalted butter
1 Tbsp. olive oil
1 tsp. minced garlic
⅓ cup double-smoked bacon (optional)
1 Tbsp. finely diced leek
1 Tbsp. finely diced carrots
1 Tbsp. finely diced onions
1 cup shiitake mushrooms, stemmed
   and sliced ¼-inch thick
3 Tbsp. vegetable or chicken stock
   (see page 170 or 169)
1 Tbsp. unsalted butter
¼ tsp. very finely chopped fresh rosemary
1 Tbsp. finely chopped tomato,
   peeled and seeded

ABOUT THE RECIPE: I think dried beans need a lot of other flavors to make them interesting. This dish works for me because of the strength of the mushroom stock and bacon flavors. We sometimes use a meat element in our vegetarian menu, because a lot of the people who order it aren't strict vegetarians. For those who are, the meat can be left out.

TO PREPARE BEANS: Rinse the soaked beans separately under cold water, drain and place them in separate pots in enough cold water to cover. Bring to a boil. Remove and discard any beans that come to the surface. Drain the beans and run under cold water until cool. Return the beans to separate pots; add half the stock to each and add enough water to cover.

Add leek, carrot and onion to each of the pots and slowly bring to a simmer. Skim and discard any beans that rise to the top. Simmer the beans for approximately 1 hour until tender. The beans can be cooked up to 1 day ahead and refrigerated.

EMULSION: Bring the mushroom stock to a boil, turn down to a simmer and reduce by half. Add the wine and reduce by half again. Whisk in butter. Reserve, keeping warm.

CASSOULET: Heat 1 tsp. butter with oil in a small casserole over medium heat. Add garlic, bacon, leek, carrots and onions and sauté for 1 minute. Add the mushrooms and sweat for 2–3 minutes. Add the precooked beans, stock and the remaining 1 Tbsp. butter. Season with salt and freshly ground white pepper. Add rosemary. Cover and simmer for 1–2 minutes until warmed through. Add the diced tomato and keep warm.

TO ASSEMBLE: Before serving, heat the emulsion over medium heat. On 4 large plates, place a portion of the cassoulet mixture. Spoon emulsion around beans and serve immediately.

WINE: A big, spicy Chateauneuf-du-Pape fits the bill, as does a big Pinot Noir.

Serves 4

Seared Alaskan scallops with a saffron-vanilla cream

CREAM
¼ cup chicken stock
    (see page 169)
½ tsp. saffron threads
¼ cup heavy cream
pulp of ½ vanilla bean
2 Tbsp. unsalted butter

SCALLOPS
1–2 Tbsp. vegetable oil
8 large Alaskan scallops

SPINACH
1 Tbsp. unsalted butter
½ lb. spinach, washed, dried and
    de-stemmed

lemon juice, to taste

ABOUT THE RECIPE: Vanilla adds a touch of natural sweetness to balance out the rich flavor of scallops. The saffron counteracts by adding a bit of bitterness to balance out the sweetness of the cream sauce. This is one of those natural flavor combinations. It also works beautifully with lobster.

TO PREPARE CREAM: In a small saucepan, mix stock and saffron threads, and simmer over medium heat to reduce by half. In a separate pot, heat cream and reduce by one-third. Strain in the saffron stock. Add vanilla pulp. Bring to a simmer and swirl until the vanilla has been incorporated into the sauce. Remove from heat, whisk in butter. Season with salt. Set aside and keep warm.

SCALLOPS: Preheat the oven to 375° F. Heat a nonstick pan over medium-high heat and add the oil. Season the scallops on both sides with fine sea salt and freshly ground white pepper. When the oil is lightly smoking, place the scallops in the pan. Sear until the scallops are golden, turn and sear the other side; 1–2 minutes per side. Place pan in oven. Roast 2–3 minutes in the oven for medium rare.

SPINACH: In a large nonstick pan, melt the butter over medium heat and add the spinach. Sauté until wilted, and season with salt and freshly ground white pepper.

TO ASSEMBLE: Heat the saffron-vanilla cream slightly. It is very important to have a proper balance of acidity, so add a little lemon juice to taste just before serving.

To serve, divide spinach among 4 plates, place 1 scallop on top and lean a second against the first. Spoon saffron-vanilla cream around each plate.

WINE: A big Californian or Australian Chardonnay.

Serves 4

Seared Alaskan scallops with
a saffron-vanilla cream (facing)

Butter-braised Atlantic lobster with leek ravioli and a red beet and horseradish sauce

LOBSTERS

2 qts. water

⅓ cup white wine vinegar

3 Tbsp. coarse sea salt or kosher salt

four 1-lb. Atlantic lobsters

RAVIOLI

1 Tbsp. olive oil

2 shallots, finely chopped

½ tsp. minced garlic

2 cups thinly sliced leek greens, washed

½ cup heavy cream

2 Tbsp. mascarpone cheese

¼ recipe pasta dough (see page 173)

SAUCE

1 medium red beet

2 Tbsp. balsamic vinegar

¼ cup chicken stock (see page 169)

juice of ½ lemon

1 tsp. creamed horseradish

2½ cups beurre monté (see page 172)

parsley oil (see page 171) for garnish

ABOUT THE RECIPE: My buddy Dave, of Deluxe Seafood, has a brother who operates a fishery on the East Coast and they deal directly so I know their lobsters are 100% fresh and delivered within 24 hours of being trapped in Nova Scotia waters.

I provided my brother David with this recipe for his Millennium New Year's dinner, and he received rave reviews. The finishing liquid is a rich butter sauce, making this a very rich dish, but the end result is fantastic! If my brother can do it, so can you.

TO PREPARE LOBSTERS: Poaching the lobsters can be done ahead of time. Combine water, white wine vinegar and salt and bring to a boil. Cook each lobster separately. Plunge the lobster into the boiling water and cook for 2 minutes. Do not overcook since the meat should be rare. When the lobster is done, immerse in an ice bath until cooled. Remove and allow to rest.

Remove the meat from the tail and claw sections. The best way to remove the under-cooked meat from the shell is to crack the shell rather than cutting it. Wrap the tail in a towel, turn it on its side and crack it by pressing down on it. For claws, remove the smaller pincer by wiggling it free, then crack the claw with the back of a heavy knife. You can reserve the carcasses and use them for another recipe.

RAVIOLI: In a large sauté pan, heat the oil over medium heat. Add shallots and sweat uncovered for 1–2 minutes. Add garlic and leek greens, and sweat uncovered until almost soft. Add cream and reduce until it just coats the leek greens. Remove from heat and allow to cool. When leek mixture is cooled, add mascarpone and mix well. Season with salt and freshly ground white pepper, cover and refrigerate until ready to use.

To make ravioli, follow method on page 173.

SAUCE: Combine beet, balsamic vinegar and stock in pot and simmer for 5 minutes. Transfer to blender or food processor and purée. Press through a fine-mesh sieve. Place purée in small pot and add the lemon juice and horseradish. Set aside.

TO ASSEMBLE: Place the beurre monté over medium heat. Make sure it does not boil as it will separate. Put the rare lobster meat into the butter and leave for 5–6 minutes.

Meanwhile, reheat the ravioli in a separate pot of boiling salted water. Drain and toss with a small amount of the beurre monté, salt and freshly ground white pepper until well coated.

Bring the beet sauce to a simmer and season with salt and possibly more lemon juice. Add a bit of beurre monté gradually, stirring until the beet sauce coats the back of a metal spoon. Keep warm.

To serve, spoon some of the beet sauce onto 4 plates. Remove the lobster from the butter with a slotted spoon. Place lobster meat on top of beet sauce. Top with one of the ravioli and drizzle with a spoonful of beurre monté. Garnish with a touch of parsley oil around the beet sauce.

WINE: A rich Riesling; otherwise a very solid white Burgundy or white-style Bordeaux.

Serves 4

Warm Yukon Gold blinis
with osetra caviar (page 138)

Seared Alaskan scallops and poached Pearl Bay oysters with a hijiki and soy-ginger broth

BROTH

2 Tbsp. hijiki (available at specialty
Asian or Japanese food stores)

⅔ cup chicken stock (see page 169)

½ tsp. ginger, minced

⅔ cup heavy cream

1 tsp. light soy sauce

NAPA CABBAGE

1½ cups julienned napa cabbage

1 Tbsp. unsalted butter

½ tsp. minced shallots

¼ tsp. minced garlic

½ tsp. rice vinegar

SEAFOOD

1 Tbsp. canola oil

4 large Alaskan scallops, rinsed,
cleaned and dried

½ cup dry white wine

4 medium fresh Pearl Bay oysters

ABOUT THE RECIPE: People sometimes wonder why a restaurant with its roots in the French classics would feature Asian flavors like hijiki. To me it's not odd at all. For one thing, I grew up next door to a Japanese family and my palate is accustomed to those flavors. For another, France and Japan have a lot in common in their attitude toward food. Both respect the ingredients above everything else, and both like clean flavors. In the top restaurants in France, we're now beginning to see a few Asian influences.

TO PREPARE BROTH: Place hijiki in a small bowl, add 1 cup cold water and set aside. In a saucepan over medium heat, bring the stock to a boil with the ginger. Lower heat and simmer for 5 minutes. Steep 5 more minutes, strain, reserving stock. Add cream and soy sauce; bring just to a boil. Remove from heat and set aside.

NAPA CABBAGE: Bring a large pot of salted water to a boil. Blanch cabbage until tender, 1–2 minutes. Plunge into ice water to stop cooking. Drain well and dry with paper towels.

In a nonstick skillet, heat the butter over medium heat. Sauté shallots and garlic for 1 minute. Add cabbage, season with salt and freshly ground white pepper, and sauté for 1 minute. Finish with rice vinegar. Keep warm.

SEAFOOD: Preheat oven to 375° F. Heat oil in an ovenproof nonstick pan over medium-high heat. Season the scallops with salt and freshly ground white pepper. Sear scallops on 1 side until golden brown. Turn scallops over and place pan in oven for 3 minutes or until scallops are warmed through. Do not overcook. Remove scallops from oven and keep warm.

TO ASSEMBLE: Strain the hijiki. Bring the soy-ginger broth to a boil again, and add rehydrated hijiki to the broth.

In a small saucepan, heat wine to a slow simmer. Add the oysters and poach them for 1 minute. Remove from liquid.

To serve, divide the napa cabbage among 4 large soup plates. Place a scallop on top followed by an oyster. Spoon broth over the seafood and serve immediately.

WINE: A demi-sec Vouvray or rich Chenin Blanc.

Serves 4

Skate wings with a browned butter sauce

SKATE WINGS
4 cups court bouillon (see page 170)
four 4-oz. portions skate wings, bone on

SAUCE
¼ lb. unsalted butter (½ cup)
½ cup chicken stock (see page 169)
juice of ½ lemon
1 lemon, peeled and segmented,
   segments cut in half

SPINACH
1 Tbsp. unsalted butter
1 lb. spinach, de-stemmed, rinsed and dried

3 Tbsp. capers, rinsed
fleur de sel for garnish

ABOUT THE RECIPE: In Europe and on the East Coast, skate is highly respected. So why is that? Here it's a secondary catch, and fishermen usually throw it back if they catch it.

This is the classic recipe that you'll find all over France. You don't need to do anything different with it. It's one of my favorites because of its simplicity.

TO PREPARE SKATE WINGS: In a large saucepan, bring the court bouillon to a simmer. Add the skate wings and poach until ridges begin to separate. Be careful not to overcook or the fish will become tough and dry. Remove from poaching liquid and cut fish from the bone.

SAUCE: In a heavy saucepan over medium heat, melt the butter and boil until it starts to turn light brown. Whisk occasionally, watching carefully so butter does not burn. When it turns dark brown and has a nutty aroma, remove from heat.

In a separate saucepan, simmer stock to reduce by half. Remove from heat. Gradually whisk in browned butter to emulsify. Add lemon juice and whisk. Add lemon segments and keep warm but do not allow to boil or the sauce may separate.

SPINACH: In another saucepan, heat the butter over medium heat, add spinach, and sweat for 2–3 minutes. Season with salt and freshly ground white pepper and keep warm.

TO ASSEMBLE: Arrange some spinach in the middle of each serving plate. Place the skate on top (the fish can be reheated in poaching liquid, if necessary). Stir capers into browned butter sauce and spoon over and around the fish. Sprinkle with a pinch of fleur de sel.

WINE: A Pouilly-Fuissé or a lovely Mâcon Chardonnay.

Serves 4

Seared halibut with a kumquat and cumin beurre blanc

VEGETABLES
3 Tbsp. unsalted butter
¼ cup diced carrots
¼ cup diced parsnips
¼ cup diced celeriac
½ cup chicken stock (see page 169)
3 sprigs thyme
1 clove garlic, crushed

BEURRE BLANC
1 shallot, finely diced
1 cup dry white wine
⅓ cup rice vinegar

½ cup unsalted butter, cubed
½ tsp. ground cumin
pinch of cayenne
2 whole fresh kumquats, finely minced
juice of ½ lime

HALIBUT
1 Tbsp. vegetable oil
four 2-oz. halibut portions,
    skin on, scaled

pinch of fleur de sel for garnish

ABOUT THE RECIPE: Several years ago I was sous-chef at Cherrystone Cove in Gastown, one of the top restaurants of its time in Vancouver. This dish came out of some experiments I did with whole kumquats very finely cut up. With most seafood you need a balance of acid, and lemon usually provides it. Kumquat, with its extra sweetness and sharpness, adds more complexity. Another showstopper dish.

TO PREPARE THE VEGETABLES: In a small pan, melt 2 Tbsp. butter over medium heat. Add carrots and sauté 2–3 minutes. Add parsnip and celeriac and sauté a further 3 minutes. Add stock, thyme, garlic and remaining butter and bring to a simmer. Simmer until stock is reduced and vegetables nicely glazed. Remove thyme and garlic clove and season with salt and freshly ground white pepper. Keep warm.

BEURRE BLANC: Combine shallots, wine and vinegar and reduce to a syrup. Slowly whisk in butter over low heat (add a touch of cream if you are nervous that the sauce will separate). Add cumin, cayenne, kumquats, lime juice and salt and freshly ground white pepper to taste. Keep warm.

HALIBUT: Preheat oven to 375° F. Heat the oil in a nonstick pan over medium-high heat. Season halibut on both sides with salt and freshly ground white pepper. Sear the halibut skin-side down until crisp. For a nicely seared skin, make sure your pan is quite hot so the skin gets crispy rather than boiling in its own juices. Turn halibut over and place in oven for 2–3 minutes.

TO ASSEMBLE: Divide glazed vegetables among 4 plates. Place halibut on top, skin-side up. Pour beurre blanc around vegetables and finish fish with a pinch of fleur de sel. Serve immediately.

WINE: An exotic, rich white Viognier, off-dry Chenin or Muscat.

Serves 4

Poulet rôti à la grand-mère

ROAST CHICKEN

one 6–7 lb. free-range roasting
   chicken
1 lemon, quartered
1 head garlic, sliced in
   half horizontally
2–3 sprigs thyme
¼ cup unsalted butter, softened
¼ cup dry white wine
1 cup chicken stock
   (see page 169)

GARLIC POTATOES

12 small potatoes
1 head garlic, separated into cloves, skin on
vegetable oil
fleur de sel or coarse sea salt

GREEN BEANS

1 Tbsp. unsalted butter
1 tsp. finely chopped shallots
¼ lb. thin green beans, trimmed
   and blanched

ABOUT THE RECIPE: This is a mother's mother's recipe—I don't think anyone can go wrong. Outside of having an excellent aged piece of beef on its own, if you want to make me a happy man you roast a chicken in this way and serve it to me with a big glass of Burgundy. If it's a great bird, properly seasoned and properly roasted, it's elegant.

TO PREPARE ROAST CHICKEN: Preheat oven to 375° F. Clean and dry chicken inside and outside. Season inside with salt and freshly ground white pepper. Place lemon, garlic and thyme inside cavity of chicken. Truss with butcher's twine. Season butter with salt and freshly ground white pepper. Brush onto breasts and legs. Refrigerate chicken for 10 minutes and repeat coating of butter; refrigerate for another 10 minutes. Discard any leftover butter.

Place chicken on a wire rack in a large roasting pan on the middle rack of the oven. Roast for 1½–2 hours, basting every 15 minutes with pan juices. Remove from oven, check to ensure liquid inside cavity is clear. Turn chicken breast-side down on the rack and allow to cool for ½ hour. Separate breast meat and legs from carcass. Cover with foil and keep warm. Chop carcass into small pieces and reserve.

Degrease the roasting pan. Deglaze with wine and stock; bring to a boil over medium heat. Pour liquid into a large saucepan with the carcass and the flavorings from inside the cavity. Bring to a boil and reduce by half. Strain and keep warm.

POTATOES: Toss potatoes and garlic with enough oil to coat lightly. Place on baking sheet. Season with coarse salt and freshly ground white pepper. Roast until potatoes are fork tender and garlic is soft and golden.

BEANS: In a medium skillet over medium heat, melt butter and sauté shallots until transparent. Add green beans and toss to warm through.

TO ASSEMBLE: Add potatoes and roasted garlic to beans and shallots, and toss to combine. To serve, separate thigh and drumstick portions of legs and cut breasts in half. Place vegetable mixture in the middle of a platter and arrange chicken over top. Serve the jus separately in a sauce boat.

WINE: A Burgundy.

Serves 4

Squab wrapped in potato with seared foie gras,
squab jus and a garlic froth (page 110)

Côte de boeuf and braised short ribs with a celeriac purée

SHORT RIBS

2 lbs. beef short ribs, cut 1¾ inches thick
2 Tbsp. vegetable oil
3 shallots, finely chopped
6 cloves garlic, crushed
½ cup ruby port wine
1 cup dry red wine
2 or 3 cups veal stock (see page 167)
12 whole black peppercorns
8 sprigs thyme
2 bay leaves

CÔTE DE BOEUF

1 double-cut rib steak, trimmed of
    all visible fat
vegetable oil
4 tsp. unsalted butter, melted
sea salt

CELERIAC PURÉE

2 cups celeriac, peeled and diced
1 clove garlic
¼ cup heavy cream

ABOUT THE RECIPE: People have been looking for lean cuts of meat lately, but the leaner the meat the less flavor it has. When you're buying a côte de boeuf, look for good marbling. There's no point in going to all this trouble for meat that doesn't taste like much.

Look also for dry-aged beef. Dry aging the beef (hanging it) starts to break down some enzymes, and that's what gives you meat that melts in your mouth.

This is a wonderfully hearty winter dish, yet it's elegant at the same time. And there's a bonus. Any leftover short-rib jus can be used in other dishes, or saved and used again for braising short ribs.

TO PREPARE SHORT RIBS: Preheat oven to 350° F. Trim excess fat from short ribs. Sprinkle both sides of ribs with salt and freshly ground white pepper.

In a Dutch oven, heat oil over medium-high heat. Add ribs and brown on all sides for 5–7 minutes. Transfer ribs to plate; set aside. Remove all but 1 Tbsp. fat from pan.

Reduce heat to medium and add shallots and garlic to Dutch oven. Cook, covered, for 2 minutes. Add port and wine and stir to deglaze bottom of pan. Add stock, peppercorns, thyme, bay leaf and browned ribs, and bring to a boil. Transfer pan to oven for 4–5 hours, or until meat is falling off the bone, turning meat occasionally. Remove pan from oven and allow to cool somewhat. Remove meat from bones and keep warm.

Strain cooking liquid into a large saucepan. Bring to a simmer and cook for 10–12 minutes, or until reduced by half (you should have about 1¾ cups). Taste and adjust seasoning.

CÔTE DE BOEUF: Before cooking the steak, let it rest in a covered pan at room temperature for approximately 1 hour.

While the celeriac is cooking, wrap the protruding steak bone in aluminum foil. Heat ⅛ inch of oil in a heavy ovenproof pan over high heat. Add the steak and sear for 4–5 minutes or until dark brown and crusty on the bottom.

Pour off most of the oil and add the butter to the pan. Place the pan in the oven and roast for about 5 minutes. Baste the meat with the butter and pan juices, turn the steak over and sprinkle with salt. Continue to cook, basting every 5 minutes for a total of 20–25 minutes, or until the meat thermometer reaches 115° F for rare. Another way to determine if the meat is cooked is to pierce the meat in the center with a cold knife or a metal skewer and leave it for 4–5 seconds, then hold to the tip of your lip; if it is warm the meat is done. Remove from the oven and let the meat rest for approximately 10 minutes.

CELERIAC PURÉE: In a medium pot, place celeriac and garlic. Cover with salted water. Bring to a boil and cook until celeriac is fork tender. Drain.

In a separate pot, heat cream. Combine celeriac, garlic and hot cream in blender and purée until smooth. Season with salt and freshly ground white pepper. Pass purée through a fine-mesh sieve. Keep warm.

TO ASSEMBLE: Before serving, return short rib meat to sauce and re-warm over low heat. Remove the string from the steak, slice the meat against the grain into 1-inch slices. Reheat celeriac purée in microwave, if necessary.

To serve, place short rib meat on plates and overlap the steak slices on top. Spoon some of the short rib jus over. Place some celeriac purée alongside.

WINE: A big, special Bordeaux, Californian or Australian Cabernet, or a big old Chilean.

Serves 4

Poached smoked sablefish salad with baby
wild greens, Rose potatoes and a horseradish
and grainy mustard vinaigrette (page 134)

Pancetta-wrapped rabbit loin
with couscous in a squab jus

RABBIT

2 large rabbit loins (at least 6 inches long)

6 thin slices Italian pancetta

2 Tbsp. vegetable oil

2 Tbsp. unsalted butter

SQUAB JUS

1 cup squab jus (see page 110)

2 cloves garlic, lightly crushed

1 Tbsp. unsalted butter

juice of ¼ lemon

COUSCOUS

1 Tbsp. finely chopped carrots

1 Tbsp. finely chopped leeks

1 Tbsp. finely chopped celery

1 cup cooked Israeli couscous

   (see page 106)

ABOUT THE RECIPE: Rabbit tends to have a strong flavor, and in North America a lot of people have trouble with it. Here, pancetta makes it more appealing and approachable by adding a complementary flavor element.

TO PREPARE RABBIT: Season the rabbit loins with freshly ground white pepper. Arrange 2–3 slices pancetta on a work surface, overlapping the slices so they are the length of the loin. Lay the seasoned rabbit loin across the pancetta, roll up and tie with kitchen string or butcher twine. Repeat with the other loin. Set aside.

Preheat oven to 350° F. Heat the oil in an ovenproof nonstick skillet over medium-high heat. When hot, sear the pancetta-wrapped loin on all sides. Transfer to the preheated oven for 5–6 minutes, turning occasionally. The loin should be medium rare or pinkish inside. If you want the rabbit cooked a little more, place in the oven for a further 2–3 minutes.

Remove loins from the oven. Place 1 Tbsp. of the butter in the pan to melt, and coat the loins. Transfer the loins to a plate, cover with foil to keep warm.

SQUAB JUS: Degrease the same pan. Deglaze with squab jus and simmer with garlic until reduced by half. Remove garlic. Whisk in butter, season with salt and lemon juice to taste.

COUSCOUS: In a separate pan over medium heat, heat remaining 1 Tbsp. of butter. Add carrots and sauté for 1 minute. Add leeks and celery and sauté for a further 1 minute. Add couscous and toss to warm through. Season with salt and freshly ground pepper.

TO ASSEMBLE: Remove string and cut the loins into 4 portions. Divide the couscous mixture among 4 individual bowls. Arrange loins on top and spoon some of the jus around the couscous. Serve immediately.

WINE: A Burgundy or a big, rich Pinot Noir.

Serves 4

Sainte Maure de Touraine cheese with dates

8 Medjool dates, pits removed
four 1-oz. portions Sainte Maure de
    Touraine cheese, straw removed

ABOUT THE RECIPE: This Loire Valley goat cheese has a lovely walnut smell. Simple dates are gorgeous with it, particularly the succulent Medjool variety.

TO ASSEMBLE: Arrange dates and cheese on 4 serving plates.

WINE: An off-dry Vouvray from right next door to where the cheese is made.

Serves 4

Roquefort cheese with caramelized pears and cilantro

2 tsp. vegetable oil
2 Anjou pears, skinned, cored and cut in
    medium dice
1 tsp. unsalted butter

2 Tbsp. brown sugar
¼ tsp. cracked black pepper
3 tsp. julienned cilantro
four 1-oz. portions Roquefort cheese

ABOUT THE RECIPE: There are a lot of different kinds of Roquefort. I prefer one that's quite creamy and just on the edge of sharpness. Choose a variety that you like.

TO PREPARE: In a skillet, heat oil over medium-high heat. Add pears and cook, gently turning occasionally, until they turn golden brown. Add butter and brown sugar and toss gently until sugar coats pears. Reduce heat to medium and add black pepper. Remove from heat and allow to cool.

To serve, mix cilantro into pears and place a small scoop of pears on 4 plates. Place the cheese on the side.

WINE: A sweet Loire white.

Serves 4

Fourme d'Ambert cheese
with candied walnuts

1 cup walnut halves
sugar
¼ cup water
½ tsp. sea salt

¼ tsp. freshly ground white pepper
four 1-oz. portions Fourme
    d'Ambert cheese

ABOUT THE RECIPE: This is very mild for a blue-veined cheese. The word *fourme* comes from the Latin *forma* meaning form or shape. The Italian *formaggio* comes from the same root, and so, probably, does *fromage*.

TO PREPARE: Preheat oven to 325° F. Spread the walnuts on a baking sheet and toast in the oven until golden brown. Remove and allow to cool.

Weigh walnuts and multiply weight by 4. This number is the weight of sugar you will need to use. In a heavy saucepan, combine the sugar and water. Warm over medium heat until it becomes syrupy and forms a 2-inch thread when lifted. Stir in nuts, salt and freshly ground white pepper, and continue cooking until sugar starts to caramelize. Immediately spread out onto a parchment-lined baking sheet. When cool, break and separate nuts.

To serve, place a portion of cheese onto each serving plate and garnish with a small amount of the walnuts.

WINE: Sauternes, Muscat, Beaumes-de-Venise or Rivesault.

Serves 4

The cheese course

Cheese became a part of my life when I was an exchange student in Scandinavia. Every morning began with hearty breads, Earl Grey tea and a block of nutty Jarlsberg. Then, on a trip to Europe with my best friend in 1985, I discovered real brie and camembert. I returned home a convert, but I realized to my chagrin that although the cheese course is an important aspect of any fine meal in Europe, North Americans look at it with suspicion.

For many of my guests, even now, I almost have to force the issue. The French *chariot des fromages*, stacked with dozens of goat, cow and sheep cheeses, would be too overpowering here. I want to introduce the cheeses, mostly French, that I love, so rather than offer a selection, I put one small serving of a single cheese on a plate, with or without a garnish and usually with a piece of dense fruit-and-nut bread. The cheese doesn't have to be ordered as something special or chosen from among a whole confusing array—it's just a natural part of the progression of the meal.

In my own meals, though, I like to sit down with a whole plate of cheeses and a bottle of wine and just indulge.

< *Reblochon cheese with kumquat marmalade (page 74)*

Passion fruit tart with a dark Valrhona chocolate base

CHOCOLATE BASE

4 oz. bittersweet Valrhona chocolate, chopped

2 Tbsp. cocoa powder

¼ lb. unsalted butter (½ cup)

1 cup sugar

2 large eggs

1 tsp. vanilla extract

½ cup flour, sifted

¼ tsp. salt

CUSTARD

½ cup unsalted butter

¼ cup heavy cream

3 large eggs

2 large egg yolks

½ cup sugar

¾ cup passion fruit purée (available at specialty food stores)

crème anglaise (page 178) for garnish
chocolate sauce (page 178) for garnish

ABOUT THE RECIPE: I like to use passion fruit occasionally because of that seductive flavor. This dessert is a real customer favorite, yet it's simplicity itself: passion fruit custard on a brownie. We make this in individual portions, but it can also be made in a springform pan and served in slices.

TO PREPARE CHOCOLATE BASE: Preheat oven to 350° F. Melt chocolate in a double boiler over simmering water. Whisk in the cocoa powder. When chocolate is melted, remove from double boiler and keep warm.

With an electric mixer, cream butter and sugar. Continue mixing while adding eggs one at a time. Add vanilla. Mix in flour and salt. With a spoon, fold the warm chocolate mixture into the batter and blend well.

If you are making individual servings, use an 11 x 7-inch metal pan. For a tart, use a 9-inch springform pan. Line pan with parchment. Butter and flour it. Pour batter into pan and smooth the top. Batter should be no more than 1 inch deep. Bake for 15–20 minutes, or until set. Remove from oven and cool in the pan.

CUSTARD: Heat butter and cream over double boiler and stir until blended. In a large bowl, whisk eggs and yolks over hot water until slightly warm. Slowly whisk butter mixture into eggs, followed by the sugar and purée. Place the bowl in a water bath or transfer the custard to a double boiler over barely simmering water, and stir until the spoon leaves a trail when pulled through mixture. Remove from heat and strain.

TO ASSEMBLE: Preheat oven to 250° F. For individual servings, cut chocolate base into six 3-inch rounds. Use a separate cutter for each tart so that you can leave the base in the cutters, using them as a mold. Place the cutters on a parchment-lined baking sheet and fill to the top with the custard.

For springform tart, remove the chocolate base from pan and discard parchment. Wash sides of pan. Dry thoroughly and replace chocolate base. Pour in custard and smooth the top. Place pan on a baking sheet. Bake for 20 minutes for individual rounds or 20–30 minutes for springform pan. Remove from oven and run sharp knife around edge to keep custard from sticking to sides of pan or molds—this will prevent cracks in the filling. Cool at room temperature, then cover and refrigerate overnight.

Before serving, run a knife around edges of molds or pan and remove desserts. Sprinkle custard evenly with granulated sugar and caramelize with small torch.

Serve with crème anglaise and chocolate sauce, or simply on its own.

WINE: Banyuls, or, for the bloody-minded, a sparkling Shiraz. But a chilled eau de vie would also be lovely.

Serves 6 to 12 · photo, page 120

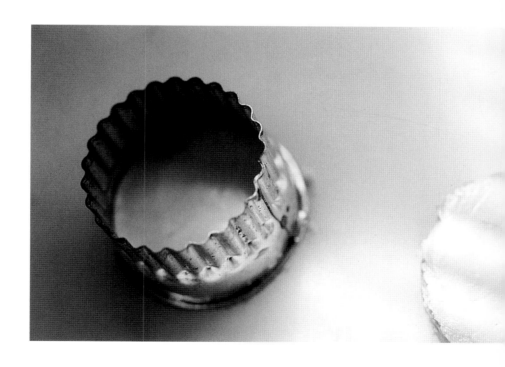

Walnut cake with maple ice cream (facing)

Walnut cake with maple ice cream

ICE CREAM

1 cup heavy cream

1 cup whole milk

5 large egg yolks

⅓ cup sugar

⅓ cup maple syrup

WALNUT CAKE

1½ cups flour

1 tsp. baking powder

¾ cup maple syrup

juice of 1 lemon

¾ lb. unsalted butter,
    room temperature (1½ cups)

1¼ cup sugar

pulp of ½ vanilla bean

7 large eggs

1 cup walnut pieces, toasted, ground

ABOUT THE RECIPE: The cake is another of Mom's recipes. When I was younger, I was known to come home from school and eat an entire cake. The maple ice cream was my addition, and Mom approves.

TO PREPARE ICE CREAM: In a saucepan over medium-high heat bring cream and milk almost to boiling point. In a bowl, whisk yolks and sugar to the ribbon stage. Add maple syrup. Temper the yolk mixture with some of the cream and milk. Finish whisking in remaining cream and milk. Place mixture in a double boiler over simmering water and stir constantly until it reaches 175° F or it coats the back of a spoon. Cool and strain. Freeze in an ice cream maker according to instructions. (The ice cream will be more velvety if the mixture is refrigerated overnight.)

WALNUT CAKE: Line terrine molds or loaf pans with parchment and grease with butter and dust with flour. Preheat oven to 325° F. Sift together flour and baking powder and set aside. Combine maple syrup and lemon juice and set aside. With an electric mixer, cream together butter, sugar and vanilla pulp. Add one egg at a time to the butter mixture until well blended. Add half of the flour mixture and beat to incorporate. Beat in half of maple syrup mixture. Repeat, beating in flour then maple syrup mixture. Scrape down the bowl.

Add ground walnuts; mix until just combined. Pour batter into prepared pans. Bake for 45–60 minutes, or until a knife inserted in the middle comes out clean.

WINE: Vin Santo.

Serves 8

Apple galette with fennel ice cream

ICE CREAM

2 bulbs fennel, trimmed

1 cup heavy cream

1 cup whole milk

pulp of 1 large vanilla bean

5 large egg yolks

½ cup sugar

FRANGIPANE

6 Tbsp. unsalted butter

¼ cup confectioners' sugar

¾ cup ground blanched almonds

2 Tbsp. all-purpose flour

1 whole egg, lightly beaten

GALETTE

1 sheet frozen puff pastry, thawed

2 Granny Smith apples, peeled and cored

2 Tbsp. melted unsalted butter

2 tsp. granulated sugar

1 tsp. ground cinnamon

CARAMEL SAUCE

1¼ cups granulated sugar

2 Tbsp. water

2 cups heavy cream

2 Tbsp. unsalted butter

powdered sugar for dusting

ABOUT THE RECIPE: Some taste combinations are naturals, and apple and caramel is certainly one of them. This galette was the initial dessert on my menu and it continues to appear. It's my mom's favorite—a classic combination of puff pastry, frangipane, caramel and apples. If I take it off the menus, people ask for it back.

TO PREPARE ICE CREAM: Using a mandoline, slice fennel bulbs paper-thin. Combine cream, milk, fennel and vanilla pulp in a heavy saucepan. Over medium-high heat bring liquid just to boiling point.

In a stainless steel bowl, whisk yolks and sugar to a thick ribbon stage. Temper the yolk mixture by stirring in some of the hot cream-and-milk mixture. Slowly add the remaining hot cream mixture. Place mixture in a double boiler over simmering water and stir constantly until it reaches 175° F. Remove from heat. Strain and cool. Refrigerate overnight. Freeze in ice cream machine according to manufacturer's directions.

FRANGIPANE: Beat butter and sugar together until smooth. Add almonds and flour; mix well. Slowly add egg and mix until well incorporated. Refrigerate until ready to use.

GALETTE: Preheat oven to 400° F. Cut puff pastry with a 4-inch round cookie cutter. (The pastry will cut more easily if it is frozen, so if possible, roll out and freeze on a baking sheet before cutting.) Roll puff pastry to ¼-inch thickness. Use a smaller round cutter to imprint a guideline for the apples, leaving a ½-inch border. After cutting, chill for 1 hour. Slice apples thinly, about ⅛-inch thick. Place 1 Tbsp. frangipane in the middle of puff pastry round and press gently to even the top. Carefully place apple slices around the frangipane in a fan pattern.

Drizzle melted butter over apples; be careful not to let butter melt over sides of puff pastry. Sprinkle with a mixture of the sugar and cinnamon. Place on parchment-lined baking sheet; bake for 10–15 minutes or until puff pastry is golden brown on bottom and apples are cooked.

CARAMEL SAUCE: In a heavy-bottomed pot, boil the sugar with the water until it turns dark brown. Carefully stir in the cream (it might bubble up). Remove from heat. Stir in the butter.

TO ASSEMBLE: Galettes can be served right away or cooled and reheated for a few minutes in medium oven before serving. To serve, place apple galette in center of plate. Dust with confectioners' sugar and place a scoop of ice cream on top. Drizzle caramel sauce around the galette. Serve immediately.

WINE: A Bonnezeaux or any sweet Chenin Blanc.

Serves 4 to 6 · photo, page 116

{ B A S I C S }

LEARNING TO SEASON in cooking is like learning to stickhandle in hockey; it's absolutely

fundamental. And yet it's one of the most common things for cooks to forget. Because every-

body's preference is different, I seldom specify quantities of salt and pepper in the ingredient

lists, but I always specify when salt and pepper should be added.

Good unprocessed sea salt will make a tremendous difference to your cooking. It com-

pares to table salt the way that tap water compares to spring water. We use the French fleur

de sel, but there are many other varieties available, each subtly different. Pepper should

always be freshly ground because it loses its essential oils when exposed to air. I usually use

white pepper. It has a gentler flavor than black pepper and it's invisible in most dishes. Still,

there are times when nothing but the assertive look and taste of black pepper will do. Add

lemon juice, vinegar or another acid just before serving to brighten flavors.

Fish stocks

As with any stock, fish stocks depend on extremely fresh, extremely clean bones. If the smell of the bones is a bit off, do not use them. The bones need to be as fresh as the fish.

Make sure the bones are well rinsed with extremely cold water to ensure there is no blood remaining on them. Do not cook them longer than 20 minutes once they come to a simmer or they will taste too fishy. You're going for a nice neutral flavor, but if you cook them too long the stock gets fishy and cloudy.

FISH FUMET

2 lbs. bones of raw white fish
2 Tbsp. vegetable oil
1 medium onion, peeled and thinly sliced
¼ bulb fennel, thinly sliced
1 leek, white part only, thinly sliced
10 white peppercorns
½ tsp. fine sea salt
1 sprig flat-leaf parsley
1 bay leaf
1 cup dry white wine
8 cups water

Under slow-running cold water, rinse the bones until the water is clear. Pat dry and cut into 4-inch pieces. Heat the oil in a large stockpot over medium heat. Add the onion, fennel, leek, peppercorns, salt, parsley and bay leaf. Turn the heat to medium-low and cook the vegetables until soft. Add the bones and cook for about 8–10 minutes, stirring occasionally.

Add wine and water and bring to a boil. Reduce heat to a gentle boil for 10 minutes only, skimming off any foam that rises to the top. Remove from the heat and let rest for 10 minutes.

Strain the fish fumet through a fine-mesh sieve and press the solids to extract as much flavor as possible. This stock will keep in your fridge for up to 3 days or freeze for up to 2 months.

Yields 3 cups

MUSSEL STOCK

1½ Tbsp. vegetable oil
2 large shallots, thinly sliced
1 medium clove garlic, thinly sliced
5 white peppercorns
1 sprig flat-leaf parsley
1 sprig fresh thyme
1 bay leaf
¼ cup white wine
3 lbs. mussels, cleaned, beards
    removed and well rinsed

If you're not allergic to shellfish, this is a more intense alternative to the fish fumet. All the liquid comes from the mussels.

Heat the oil in a large pot over medium-high heat. Add the shallots, garlic, peppercorns, parsley, thyme and bay leaf and sauté until shallots and garlic are soft, 3–4 minutes. Add the wine to the pot along with the mussels and cover. Cook, stirring occasionally until the mussels are open, 2–3 minutes. Remove from heat and strain through fine-mesh sieve. Mussel meat can be cooled, then frozen in sealed freezer bags with some of the stock for up to 2 months.

Allow liquid to cool, then refrigerate. Store liquid in the fridge for up to 3 days or in the freezer for up to 2 months.

Yields 1½ cups

Veal stocks

Milk-fed bones make for a cleaner stock, but regular veal can be used. Shank bones have the most gelatin for the richest stock. These recipes can be used immediately, refrigerated for 1 week or frozen in an airtight container for up to 3 months.

VEAL STOCK

1 lb. milk-fed veal bones (shank bones
    if possible)
⅓ cup honey
⅓ cup unsalted butter
1 medium carrot, coarsely chopped
1 leek, white part only, coarsely chopped
½ medium onion, chopped
1 stalk celery, trimmed and coarsely
    chopped
5 cloves garlic, minced
1 Tbsp. tomato paste
1 ripe tomato, peeled, seeded and chopped
2 sprigs thyme
1 bay leaf

Preheat oven to 450° F. Roast bones for 30–35 minutes until lightly browned. Remove excess fat from pan and roast bones for another 10 minutes.

In a small pan over medium heat, melt honey and butter. Pour mixture over bones and roast for another 5 minutes. Transfer bones to a stockpot and set aside.

In roasting pan, place carrot, leek, onion, celery and garlic. Roast over medium-high heat on the stove or in the oven until golden brown. Add 2 cups cold water to vegetables and bring to a boil to deglaze roasting pan. Reduce by half.

Add vegetable mixture to stockpot along with tomato paste, tomato, thyme and bay leaf. Add enough cold water to cover bones. Simmer on low for 6–8 hours (do not allow stock to boil). Make sure stock ingredients are always ¾ covered with water. Frequently skim fat and impurities that rise to the top. Remove from heat and allow to cool slightly. Strain and reserve bones (see remoullage).

Yields 5 cups

REMOULLAGE

After you have prepared your veal stock, don't throw away the cooked bones. They will still have some flavor, enough for a remoullage, a second extraction of veal stock. This liquid can be used as a base instead of the cold water for your next veal stock.

Use half the quantity of vegetables called for in veal stock. Toss with enough oil to coat and roast as for veal stock. Deglaze roasting pan with a little water. Transfer to a stockpot, add reserved bones and cover with cold water. Bring to a boil, reduce heat and simmer for 45 minutes. Strain and discard vegetables and bones.

VEAL REDUCTION

¾ cups dry red wine, such as a Shiraz-
    Cabernet blend
⅓ cup port wine
½ cup shallots, finely sliced
¼ head garlic, halved
2 sprigs thyme
5 cups good quality-veal stock

In a large pot over medium heat, combine wine and port and add shallots, garlic and thyme. Reduce to a syrup. Add stock and reduce by one-third. Strain.

Yields about 3 cups

Lamb and beef stocks

LAMB OR BEEF STOCK

2 lbs. lamb or beef bones

3 medium carrots, cut in chunks

2 medium onions, cut in chunks

4 stalks celery, cut in chunks

1 head garlic, cut in half

5 sprigs thyme

1 bay leaf

10 peppercorns

Preheat oven to 450° F. Lightly grease
2 roasting pans with a bit of vegetable oil.
Roast bones in a single layer in one pan for
1–1½ hours, turning occasionally until
dark brown. In the other pan, roast carrots,
onion, celery and garlic for 45–60 minutes,
or until caramelized.

Remove fat from lamb pan. Deglaze
both pans with a little water. Transfer
contents of both pans to a stockpot along
with thyme, bay leaf and peppercorns. Add
enough cold water to cover. Over medium
heat, simmer uncovered for 3–4 hours,
skimming off impurities periodically. The
stock ingredients should always be at least
three-quarters covered by water. If the
level falls below that, add more cold water.

Remove from heat and allow to
cool slightly. Strain into a clean container,
discarding all solids. For more concentrated flavor, you can reduce the stock by
half at this point. Cool to room temperature and refrigerate. Remove fat cap
before using.

Lamb or beef stock will keep in the
refrigerator for up to 1 week and can
be frozen in an airtight container for up
to 3 months.

Yields 8 to 10 cups

SHORT STOCKS

2 tsp. vegetable oil

¼ lb. lamb or beef trimmings, fat removed

1 medium carrot, cut in chunks

½ medium onion, cut in chunks

2 stalks celery, cut in chunks

3 cloves garlic

2 sprigs thyme

1 bay leaf

2 cups veal stock (see page 167)

¼ cup red wine, optional

If you need a lamb or beef stock and there's
none on hand, you can make a fairly quick
substitute by starting with veal stock or
water and infusing the flavor you need.

Heat oil in a large pot over high heat
and brown meat trimmings. Drain off fat
and add vegetables, garlic, thyme and bay
leaf. Cook uncovered, stirring occasionally
until caramelized.

Add stock and wine and stir to deglaze
pot. Reduce heat and simmer for 1 hour,
skimming off impurities. Strain and
remove all fat. For more concentrated
flavor, reduce stock by half.

Yields 1½ cups

Chicken Stocks

Chicken stock is the foundation of so much great cooking. We start the chicken by itself and remove the impurities, then add the vegetables later. This results in a clear, clean stock. Make sure the bones are not more than 1 day old and that they do not have excess fat on them. We remove a lot of the skin to prevent too much fat.

CHICKEN STOCK

5 lbs. fresh chicken bones, backs and necks
1 large carrot, coarsely chopped
1 medium leek, white part only, finely
    chopped
1 medium onion, coarsely chopped
2 stalks celery, coarsely chopped
5 cloves garlic
2 sprigs thyme
2 bay leaves

Rinse chicken bones, backs and necks thoroughly with cold running water for 5–10 minutes until water runs clear. Cover bones with cold water in a large pot. Place over medium heat and bring to a boil. Turn heat to low and simmer for 20 minutes, frequently skimming the impurities that rise to the surface.

Add carrot, leek, onion, celery, garlic, thyme and bay leaves and simmer uncovered on low for 2 hours. To ensure a clear stock, do not allow to boil.

Remove from heat and strain through a fine-mesh sieve. Allow to cool and store in refrigerator no more than 4 days. Fat can be removed easily once the stock has been refrigerated. Chicken stock can also be stored in plastic containers or resealable freezer bags for up to 3 months.

Yields about 4 quarts

DARK CHICKEN STOCK

1 Tbsp. vegetable oil
3 lbs. chicken backs, necks and a few wings
1 medium carrot, coarsely chopped
1 medium onion, coarsely chopped
2 cloves garlic, halved
1 stalk celery, coarsely chopped
2 sprigs thyme

This works perfectly as a substitute for veal stock. Reduced, it's a great replacement for veal reduction.

Preheat oven to 450° F. In a large roasting pan, heat oil over high heat, add the chicken pieces and place in oven for 45 minutes. (Chicken bones will stick to pan and will give the stock its dark color.)

Add the carrot, onion, garlic and celery, stir with a wooden spoon and roast for another 15 minutes. Stir again. Roast for another 15 minutes.

Add thyme, cover with cold water and cook for another 20 minutes, continuing to stir until bottom of pan is clean. It's very important to make sure the bones never burn as this will make the stock bitter. Strain stock through a fine-mesh sieve. Stock can be used as is, but for more intense flavor, reduce by half over low heat.

The stock can be refrigerated for up to 1 week or frozen in an airtight container for up to 2 months.

Yields about 2½ quarts

Vegetable stocks

It's nice to use light vegetable stock in soups where you want the flavor of the ingredients to shine.

Mushroom stock is the vegetable equivalent of dark chicken stock, and we use it a lot as a base on our vegetarian menu.

VEGETABLE STOCK
1 bulb fennel, thinly sliced
1 medium onion, thinly sliced
2 stalks celery, thinly sliced
1 medium carrot, thinly sliced
1 leek, green part only, thinly sliced
1 tomato, blanched, seeded and chopped
4 cloves garlic
1 tsp. white peppercorns
3 sprigs thyme
1-inch piece ginger, sliced
5 cups water

In a large pot, combine all ingredients. Over medium heat, bring to a boil. Reduce heat to low and simmer for 30–45 minutes. Strain immediately, pressing solids gently to release as much liquid as possible.

Vegetable stock can be used immediately, refrigerated for up to 1 week or frozen for up to 2 months in an airtight container.

Yields 1 quart

MUSHROOM STOCK
2 Tbsp. vegetable oil
2 lbs. mushroom trimmings
2 cloves garlic
3 sprigs thyme
2 large shallots, finely sliced
2 cups water or chicken stock
   (see page 169)

Heat oven to 375° F. In a large pot, heat oil over medium-high heat. Add mushroom trimmings, garlic, thyme and shallots and sweat them until mushrooms are very soft. Add water or stock to cover. Bring to a boil, reduce heat and allow to simmer for 30 minutes. Remove from heat, strain and lightly press warm solids to extract as much liquid as possible. To concentrate flavor, reduce by one-third after straining.

Mushroom stock can be refrigerated for up to 1 week and frozen in an airtight container or resealable freezer bags for up to 1 month.

Yields 1 quart

COURT BOUILLON
2 Tbsp. vegetable oil
2 carrots, peeled and chopped
4 stalks celery, chopped
1 leek, washed and chopped
1 onion, peeled and chopped
1 bulb fennel, chopped
1 head garlic, halved
1-inch piece ginger, chopped
bouquet garni of parsley, thyme and
   black peppercorns
1 lemon, halved
1 orange, quartered
1 tomato, quartered
1½ qts. white wine
2½ qts. water
¼ tsp. sea salt

In a small stockpot, heat oil over medium heat. Add carrot, celery, leek, onion, fennel, garlic and ginger, reduce heat to medium-low and sweat vegetables uncovered until soft. Add remaining ingredients and simmer for 1 hour. Strain.

Yields 2½ to 3 quarts

Infused oils

People get carried away with infused oils because they look so good on the plate. They add more than color, they also add intense flavor. I usually use just one oil at a time to keep it really simple.

HERB OILS

BASIL OIL

2 cups basil leaves
1 cup grapeseed oil

CILANTRO OIL

3 Tbsp. coriander seeds,
    roasted and cooled
1 cup cilantro
½ cup flat-leaf parsley
1 cup grapeseed oil

DILL OIL

1 cup flat-leaf parsley
2 cups dill
1 cup grapeseed oil

FENNEL OIL

2 cups fennel fronds
2 cups flat-leaf parsley
½ cup dill
1 cup grapeseed oil

PARSLEY OIL

4 cups flat-leaf parsley
1 cup grapeseed oil

ROSEMARY OIL

1 cup rosemary leaves
1½ cups flat-leaf parsley
1 cup grapeseed oil

Make sure the herbs you're using are extremely fresh because you want to capture as much flavor as possible. Blanch herbs briefly in boiling water. Shock in ice water to preserve color. Dry thoroughly. Purée in blender. Add oil and incorporate. Refrigerate overnight in a stainless steel or glass bowl. Strain the next day through a cheesecloth-lined sieve.

Herb oils can be refrigerated for up to 2 months in an airtight container.

Yields 1 cup

LEMON OIL

3 large lemons, washed
2 cups grapeseed oil

Remove lemon zest and cut into julienne. Combine oil and zest in a heavy saucepan. Bring to a simmer over medium-low heat. Simmer for 2 minutes, remove from heat and allow to cool.

Place in an airtight container and refrigerate overnight. Strain through cheesecloth-lined sieve. Can be refrigerated for up to 2 months in an airtight container.

Yields 2 cups

LOBSTER OIL

2 cups grapeseed oil
½ cup coarsely diced mixed carrot, onion,
    leek and celery
2 cloves garlic, crushed
2 sprigs thyme
1 lobster carcass, coarsely chopped
½ tsp. coarse salt
1 Tbsp. tomato paste

In a large pot, heat 1 Tbsp. oil and add all the vegetables, garlic and thyme. Sweat for 3–4 minutes over medium-high heat, then add the chopped lobster carcass. Cook for another 2–3 minutes, then add salt, tomato paste and remaining oil, and simmer for 7–10 minutes. Remove from heat and let oil infuse for approximately 30 minutes.

Strain liquid through a fine-mesh sieve or cheesecloth. Store refrigerated in an airtight container for up to 2 weeks.

Yields 2 cups

Glazes, dressings and sauces

BALSAMIC GLAZE

2 cups balsamic vinegar

In a small pot over medium heat, reduce the vinegar to ½ cup. Remove from heat and allow to cool. Place in airtight glass container and refrigerate until needed.

Yields ½ cup

HOUSE VINAIGRETTE

2 tsp. Dijon mustard
3 Tbsp. red wine vinegar
3 Tbsp. sherry vinegar
1 cup grapeseed oil
juice of ½ lemon

In a mixing bowl, whisk together mustard, salt, freshly ground white pepper and vinegars. Whisking constantly, very slowly drizzle the oil into the mixture. Whisk in lemon juice, to taste. Store in the refrigerator for up to 1 week.

Yields 1⅓ cups

BEURRE MONTÉ

1 lb. unsalted butter
1 Tbsp. water

Cut butter into small cubes and let it come to room temperature. Heat water in a small saucepan over low to medium heat. When water starts to steam, whisk in the butter cubes one by one until the sauce is completely emulsified. When this is done, keep sauce in a warm place. Overheating will cause it to separate.

You can't reheat beurre monté, but you can use it as you would butter.

Yields 1½ cups

BEURRE BLANC

⅔ cup dry white wine
1 shallot, finely diced
⅓ cup rice vinegar
½ lb. cold unsalted butter, cut into
    small cubes
juice of ½ lemon

This basic white butter sauce can be a base for anything. Add herbs or spices. For lemon beurre blanc, add grated zest of 1 lemon as you're reducing the wine.

If the white wine, shallot and vinegar isn't reduced to a syrup, the butter won't bind when it's added. The heat can't be too high or the butter will separate. If you're worried about the sauce separating, you can add a spoonful of cream to stabilize it.

TO PREPARE: In a saucepan over medium heat, reduce wine, shallot and vinegar to 2 Tbsp. Strain. Over low heat, whisk in butter, cube by cube; do not allow to boil. Season with salt, freshly ground white pepper and lemon juice.

Yields 1 cup

Pasta, potatoes, and grains

PASTA DOUGH

3 cups all-purpose flour

2⅓ cups semolina

16 large egg yolks

1–3 whole large eggs

½ Tbsp. olive oil

1 egg, beaten

½ tsp. water

semolina or fine cornmeal for dusting

This egg-rich pasta dough is Alsatian in style. The recipe makes 1¼ pounds of dough, enough for 40 ravioli. Most of the recipes in the book call for ¼ of the recipe. The dough can be cut into recipe-sized portions, tightly wrapped in plastic wrap and frozen in resealable bags.

You might want to reserve the leftover egg whites for another purpose. They will keep tightly covered in the refrigerator for up to 4 days and can be frozen for up to 6 months.

TO PREPARE: Place flour, semolina and a pinch of salt in bowl of a heavy-duty mixer. On slow speed, incorporate egg yolks, one at a time, with a dough hook, followed by 1 whole egg. Test by squeezing some of the mixture in your hand. If it stays together, stop adding whole eggs. Add oil. Knead a small portion. It should form a dough that is not too wet or sticky. If mixture is too wet, add more flour.

Gently knead dough on a floured surface and form into two 3-inch-thick cylinders. Cut each into 4 equal portions, wrap in plastic wrap and allow to rest in refrigerator for 1 hour before using.

Roll according to pasta machine instructions to form thin sheets, about ¹⁄₁₆ inch thick. As sheets are rolled, cover with clean cloth to prevent drying out.

Using a ravioli mold, line one sheet of the pasta on the bottom. Add a spoonful of the filling to each mold. Beat egg and water together for egg wash and brush on the exposed pasta. Cover with top sheet of pasta and press to form ravioli, squeezing any air out. Trim off excess dough and place ravioli on a parchment-covered tray spread with semolina or fine cornmeal to prevent sticking. These can be frozen in a single layer and kept in airtight container for up to 2½ weeks.

Cook ravioli in a large pot of boiling salted water with 1 Tbsp. olive oil added.

Makes enough for 40 ravioli

BASIC GNOCCHI

2 large Yukon Gold potatoes
  (approx. 1 lb.), skins on

1 large egg yolk

¼–1 cup all-purpose flour

Place the potatoes in a pot, cover with water and bring to a boil. Simmer until fork tender. Drain potatoes when tender and remove skins when they are cool enough to handle.

Press the cooked potatoes through a ricer or coarsely grate them into a large bowl. Mix the yolk into the potatoes with a wooden spoon until well blended.

Transfer the mixture to a lightly floured surface. Knead in a small amount of flour at a time until the dough is smooth but still slightly sticky. Season with salt and freshly ground white pepper.

Before proceeding, test one small piece of the dough in a small pot of boiling salted water. If it floats to the surface, adjust seasonings and continue. If it falls apart, add a little more flour to the dough and test again.

Form the dough into 1 large log and cut into 4 sections. Roll each section into a long cigar shape about ½ inch in diameter. Cut into ½-inch pieces and delicately indent by pinching the pieces in the middle. Dust well with flour. Spread the gnocchi on a parchment-lined baking sheet and freeze. These can be frozen in resealable bags until ready to use.

To cook, bring a pot of salted water to a boil, add gnocchi and cook for 2–3 minutes or until the gnocchi begin to float to the surface. As they surface, remove with a slotted spoon and drain well. They can be tossed in a heated sauce before serving.

Serves 4 to 6

MASCARPONE RISOTTO

2 to 3 cups chicken stock (see page 169)
3 Tbsp. olive oil
2 large shallots, finely chopped
1 cup risotto rice (superfino quality such as arborio or the premium canaroli)
1 cup dry white wine
2 Tbsp. mascarpone cheese
1–2 Tbsp. freshly grated Parmesan cheese
1 Tbsp. unsalted butter
Italian white truffle (optional)

This risotto is a combination of two others I have seen in my travels, one from when I worked at Emile Jung's Au Crocodile in Strasbourg, the other a superb course I had at Thomas Keller's esteemed French Laundry in the Napa Valley. Even without the truffles, this is a good basic risotto recipe.

TO PREPARE: In a medium saucepan, heat the stock, keeping it at a gentle simmer. In a large saucepan, heat the oil over medium heat, add the shallots and sauté until translucent. Do not brown. Add the rice

and cook over medium heat for 2–3 minutes until well coated. Add the wine and stir until the liquid is absorbed.

Keep the rice simmering and add ½ cup of hot stock; stir gently until it is absorbed. Do not stir too often or you risk breaking the grains. Continue this process until the risotto has been cooking for about 12 minutes. You should have a small amount of stock left over. At this point the risotto will be al dente, moist and almost creamy.

The risotto can be made ahead of time up to this stage. If making ahead of time, transfer the risotto to a large baking sheet and allow to cool down. Refrigerate in an airtight container until needed. Skip this step if you're making it all at one time.

Over medium-low heat, continue adding the remaining hot stock a bit at a time until the rice is plump and creamy, about 15 minutes.

When the risotto is cooked, gently fold in the mascarpone, Parmesan and butter. Season with salt and freshly ground white pepper. Shave truffles finely and place on top of hot risotto.

Yields 2 to 2½ cups

PARMESAN CRISPS

Preheat oven to 375° F. For each Parmesan crisp, place 1 Tbsp. of grated Parmesan cheese onto a parchment paper-lined baking sheet. Spread to about 3 inches in diameter. Bake for 7–10 minutes or until melted and golden. Remove and cool. Store in an airtight container at room temperature for 2 days.

Sorbets and granités

Sorbets for me are as much fun as those frozen pop-ups we used to eat as kids.

People often ask why I serve sorbet after the cheese course when they're used to eating it as a palate cleanser between the fish and meat courses. In the past, flavors were heavy and robust. Over the last couple of decades, though, cuisine has become more refined and clean. You no longer want to, or need to, interrupt the flow from fish to meat and the flow of the wines.

I don't even think of sorbet as a palate cleanser anymore. It has become the overture to the dessert course. I always like to make sure something, such as a jus (see pages 178–179), accompanies the sorbet as well to make it more interesting.

SIMPLE SYRUP

5 cups sugar
3⅔ cups water
⅓ cup corn syrup

Combine ingredients and bring to a boil. Continue to boil for 2 minutes. Remove from heat, strain and cool. Store at room temperature in an airtight container.
Yields 8 cups

BASIC METHOD: SORBET

Combine all ingredients and freeze. When all ingredients are combined, freeze the sorbet in an ice cream maker according to the manufacturer's instructions. Serve this immediately, or pack in an airtight container and store in freezer for up to 1 week.

APPLE SORBET

1½ cups fresh apple juice
½ cup water
¾ cup simple syrup
juice of ½ lemon

Follow basic method. Serve with spiced apple jus.
Yields 2¾ cups

APRICOT SORBET

½ cup sugar
¾ cup water
2 large apricots, peeled, pitted and
   cut into chunks
juice of 2 limes

In a saucepan over medium heat, combine sugar with water and bring to a boil. Stir to dissolve the sugar. Remove from heat and pour into a medium bowl. Chill.

Purée apricot chunks. Stir apricot purée and lime juice into cold syrup and mix well. Freeze. Serve with apricot and lime jus.
Yields 1½ cups

BLUEBERRY SORBET

2½ cups blueberries, plus a few more
   for garnish
¼ cup granulated sugar
2 Tbsp. freshly squeezed lime juice
¼ cup simple syrup

Combine blueberries and sugar in pot. Cook over low heat, stirring occasionally, until blueberries are soft. Remove from heat. Allow to cool. Stir in lime juice and simple syrup. Purée. Pass through a fine-mesh sieve. Freeze. Serve with lemon and tarragon jus.
Yields 1½ to 1¾ cups · photo, page 76

CITRUS SORBET

½ peeled banana
½ cup fresh orange juice
½ cup fresh grapefruit juice
¼ cup fresh lime juice
¼ cup simple syrup (see page 175)

Purée banana until smooth. Add the citrus juices and process until blended. Strain. Stir in simple syrup and freeze. Serve with cardamom jus.

Yields 2 cups

LEMON OR LIME SORBET

½ cup freshly squeezed lemon or lime juice
½ – ¾ cup simple syrup (see page 175)
½ cup whole milk

Mix lemon or lime juice and ½ cup simple syrup. Taste for sweetness and add more syrup if too tart. Stir in milk and freeze. Serve with banana and vanilla jus or lavender jus.

Yields 1½ cups

LYCHEE AND CHAMPAGNE SORBET

2 cups canned lychees, drained
½ cup + 2 Tbsp. water
½ cup sugar
2 cups dry champagne
pulp of ¼ vanilla bean
juice of ½ lemon

Purée lychees in food processor or blender. Bring water and sugar to a boil. Allow to cool. Mix all ingredients in a bowl. Adjust flavor, adding more lemon juice if too sweet.

Yields 2 to 2¾ cups

PINK GRAPEFRUIT SORBET

1½ cups freshly squeezed pink grapefruit juice
½ cup simple syrup (see page 175)

Follow basic method. Serve with gin and vanilla jus.

Yields 2 cups

TANGERINE SORBET

2 cups fresh tangerine juice
½ cup simple syrup (see page 175)
juice of ½ lime

Follow basic method. Serve with hibiscus jus.

Yields 2½ cups

BASIC METHOD: GRANITÉ

Combine all ingredients and freeze. Pour the liquid into a large glass baking pan and place in the freezer. Stir with a fork several times during freezing to form a granité. This will have a somewhat coarser texture than a sorbet made in an ice cream machine.

PINK CHAMPAGNE AND CHERRY GRANITÉ

2½ cups cherries, pitted
⅔ cup + 1 Tbsp. granulated sugar
¾ cup water
½ cup rosé champagne
juice of ½ lemon

Reserve some cherries for garnish. Combine remaining cherries, sugar and water in a medium saucepan. Bring to a boil over medium heat. Stir until cherries are softened. Cool for 10 minutes. Purée until smooth. Strain. Add champagne and lemon juice and freeze.

Yields 4 cups

STRAWBERRY GRANITÉ

2 cups strawberries, cut and cleaned
¼ cup granulated sugar
3 Tbsp. fresh lemon juice
¼ cup simple syrup (see page 175)
¼ cup water

Reserve a few strawberries for garnish. Combine remaining strawberries and sugar in heavy pot. Cook over low heat until strawberries are soft. Remove from heat. Allow to cool. Stir in lemon juice, simple syrup and water. Purée and strain. Freeze.

Yields 2 cups

WATERMELON AND KAFFIR LIME GRANITÉ

⅔ cup sugar
⅔ cup water
1 cup fresh kaffir lime leaves or
 ⅓ cup dried leaves
1 stalk lemon grass, coarsely chopped
½ small watermelon, peeled, seeded
 and cut into 1-inch chunks
juice of 2 limes
small slices of watermelon for garnish

In a small saucepan over medium heat, combine sugar, water, lime leaves and lemon grass and bring to a boil, stirring until the sugar dissolves. Remove from heat and steep for 1 hour.

Purée the watermelon. Strain the sugar syrup into the purée and add the lime juice. Process or mix until well blended. Freeze as for granité.

Yields 2 to 3 cups

Dessert sauces and jus

BASIC CRÈME ANGLAISE
2 cups whole milk
pulp of 1 vanilla bean
7 egg yolks
½ cup sugar

In a saucepan over medium heat, infuse the milk with the vanilla for 5 minutes.

In a large mixing bowl, whisk yolks and sugar together until the mixture reaches the light-ribbon stage. Temper the egg and sugar mixture by whisking in a small amount of the warmed milk; slowly add the rest of the milk.

Strain through a fine-mesh sieve into the saucepan and return to heat, stirring constantly with a wooden spoon. Bring to 175° F or until the sauce coats the back of the spoon. Do not boil or overcook as it will curdle.

Immediately strain into a clean stainless steel bowl in an ice bath to stop cooking.

Yields 2½ cups

CHOCOLATE SAUCE
¾ cup whole milk
¼ cup heavy cream
4 oz. bittersweet Valrhona chocolate,
    chopped

In a small heavy pot, bring milk and cream just to a boil. Remove from heat.

Place chocolate in a small pot or the top of a double boiler. Pour in hot cream mixture a little at a time, mixing until chocolate melts. Return to heat or place over hot water in double boiler to keep warm, but do not allow to simmer.

Refrigerate extra sauce in a sealed container to reheat for later use. To reheat, stir in a touch of cream and warm over hot water in a double boiler.

Yields 1 cup

A complementary jus adds a nice edge to sorbet. I like to combine sweet with tangy, hot with cold.

JUS: BASIC METHOD
Combine all ingredients in a saucepan and bring to a boil. Remove from heat, cover and allow to steep until flavor is infused. Strain and chill.

APRICOT AND LIME JUS
1 large apricot, peeled, pitted and
    cut into chunks
⅓ cup sugar
1 cup water
juice of 2 limes
3 sprigs mint

Follow basic method, steeping for 20–30 minutes. Strain, pressing the apricot to extract as much juice as possible. Serve with apricot sorbet.

Yields 1½ cups

BANANA AND VANILLA JUS
2 cups water
½ cup granulated sugar
pulp of ½ vanilla bean
zest of 1 lime
1 banana, peeled and cut in 1-inch pieces

Follow basic method, adding banana once jus has reached a boil. Poach banana for 1 minute before removing from heat. Steep overnight. Serve with lime sorbet.

Yields 2½ cups

CARDAMOM JUS

1 cup water

¼ cup granulated sugar

3 cardamom pods, crushed

zest of 1 orange

Follow basic method. Serve with
citrus sorbet.

Yields 1¼ cups

GIN AND VANILLA JUS

2 cups water

½ cup sugar

pulp of ½ vanilla bean

gin, to taste

lemon juice, to taste

Follow basic method, adding gin once
jus is cooled and strained. Serve with
pink grapefruit sorbet.

Yields 2½ cups

HIBISCUS JUS

⅓ cup sugar

2 cups water

2½ oz. dried hibiscus flowers (about 1 cup)

Follow basic method, steeping overnight.
Serve with tangerine sorbet.

Yields 2⅓ cups

LAVENDER JUS

⅓ cup sugar

2 cups water

1½ oz. dried lavender flowers
    (about 1¼ cup)

pulp of ½ vanilla bean

lemon juice, to taste

Follow basic method, steeping overnight.
Serve with lemon sorbet.

Yields 2⅓ cups

LEMON AND TARRAGON JUS

zest and juice of 1 lemon

½ cup water

¼ cup granulated sugar

1 sprig fresh tarragon

Follow basic method. Serve with
blueberry sorbet.

Yields ¾ cup · photo, page 76

MINT JUS

2 cups water

¼ cup sugar

zest of 1 lime

zest of 1 orange

pulp of ½ vanilla bean

¾ cup fresh mint

Follow basic method, adding mint when
jus is removed from heat. Steep overnight.
Serve with strawberry granité.

Yields 2¼ cups

SPICED APPLE JUS

1 cup apple juice

½ whole star anise

½ cinnamon stick

1 cardamom pods, crushed

½ tsp. chopped candied ginger

juice of ½ lemon

sugar, to taste

Follow basic method, simmering for
3 minutes before removing from heat.
Serve with apple sorbet.

Yields 1 cup

Acknowledgments

THIS BOOK has come out of the restaurant, so first I have to thank the people who have helped make Lumière a success. I am sorry if I've missed anyone.

My staff, back and front, are a great team who have put in a vast amount of work over the years to make my vision a reality. Everyone from the dishwashers to the maître d' makes Lumière a wonderful place to be, and I am grateful for their loyalty, hard work and joie de vivre.

All of the growers and suppliers from both the west and east coasts of Canada—and some in between—provide us with unparalleled raw material to work with. Many, including Susan Davidson from Glorious Garnishes, Nattie and Gary King from Hazelmere Farms and George Walter of Walter's Exotic Meats, have become friends.

I want to thank my business partner Ken Wai for allowing me to take my vision off the ground.

Vancouver media have supported us over the years and their words have helped bring us to the attention of national and international media. Together they've put us on the map.

Cate Simpson's title is publicist, but what she really does is make my life easier.

Lumière would not have come into existence without Michel Jacob of Crocodile in Vancouver. He took me back to the basics and taught me that fundamentals and consistency are the most important things in food. He also made it possible to work with his friends and mentors, Johnny Letzer and Emile Jung in Alsace.

In North America, Charlie Trotter and Daniel Boulud are two of my biggest inspirations. Their food can bring tears to my eyes.

Steven A. Kaplan kindly introduced me to Charlie, and I was introduced to Steven by Sid and Joan Cross, who have been more than loyal customers; they have influenced the direction of the restaurant. Joan also put on her Cordon Bleu toque and tested many of the recipes for the book. Murray McMillan joined her as a civilian in the line of fire, and their input was invaluable.

Many wonderful people have helped me bring this book into being. Marnie Coldham, one of my sous-chefs, worked extremely hard to put the recipes together, test them and make them work for the home cook. It's a difficult process, and she handled it with her usual style and smarts. I think of Marnie as my little sister—she's always watching out for me.

Nathan Fong not only spent innumerable hours whipping the original manuscript into shape, he also lent his food-styling flair to the photographs. He's been a good friend and tough critic for some time. I appreciate both the friendship and the criticism.

Neil Ingram, Lumière's talented sommelier, wrote the wine suggestions throughout the book, and I thank him for his insight and infinite knowledge of wine.

John Sherlock has a remarkable eye. His photographic skill made the pictures look as good as the food tastes. The beauty of the book as a whole is due to designer Peter Cocking's talent and taste. And editor Elizabeth Wilson managed to extract the flavor of my ideas as well as performing the usual editorial duties. Douglas & McIntyre believed in the book from the beginning and kept at me to get it finished.

And now, somehow, it is. A toast to you all.

Index